First World War
and Army of Occupation
War Diary
France, Belgium and Germany

3 CAVALRY DIVISION
Divisional Troops
Signal Squadron
1 January 1915 - 31 March 1919

WO95/1146/4

The Naval & Military Press Ltd
www.nmarchive.com
Published in association with The National Archives

Published by

The Naval & Military Press Ltd

Unit 10 Ridgewood Industrial Park,

Uckfield, East Sussex,

TN22 5QE England

Tel: +44 (0) 1825 749494

www.naval-military-press.com

www.nmarchive.com

This diary has been reprinted in facsimile from the original. Any imperfections are inevitably reproduced and the quality may fall short of modern type and cartographic standards.

© Crown Copyright
Images reproduced by permission of The National Archives, London, England, 2015.

Contents

Document type	Place/Title	Date From	Date To
Heading	WO95/1146/4 3 Cavalry Division Divisional Troops Signal Squadron Sept 1914-March 1919		
Heading	1914-1919 3rd Cavalry Division 3rd Signal Squadron R.E. Sep 1914-Mar 1919		
Heading	3rd Signal Squadron R.E. 3rd Cav Div. From Sept 12th 1914 To Dec 31st 1914 To Mar 1919		
Miscellaneous		02/01/1915	02/01/1915
Heading	3rd Signal Sqdrn. R.E. 3rd Cavalry Division For January-December 1915.		
Heading	3rd Signal Squadron RE Vol II 1-31.1.15		
Heading	3rd Signal Squadron R.E 3rd Cavalry Division From January 1st To 31st 1915	02/02/1915	02/02/1915
War Diary	Hazebrouck	01/01/1915	31/01/1915
War Diary	Signal	31/01/1915	31/01/1915
Heading	3rd Signal Squadron R.E Vol III 1-28.2.15		
Miscellaneous	3rd Signal Squadron		
Diagram etc	Circuit Diagram		
War Diary	Hazebrouck	01/02/1915	03/02/1915
War Diary	Ypres	04/02/1915	13/02/1915
War Diary	Hazebrouck	14/02/1915	28/02/1915
Heading	3rd Signal Squadron R.E. For The Month Of 3rd Cavalry Division March 1915 Vol IV		
War Diary	Hazebrouck	01/03/1915	11/03/1915
War Diary	Merville	11/03/1915	13/03/1915
War Diary	Hazebrouck	14/03/1915	31/03/1915
Diagram etc	Circuit Diagram		
Heading	3rd Signal Squadron R.E. Vol V 1.4-31.5.15		
Miscellaneous	3rd Signal Sqdn' R.E.		
War Diary	Hazebrouck	01/04/1915	23/04/1915
War Diary	Abeele	23/04/1915	24/04/1915
War Diary	Westoutre	24/04/1915	25/04/1915
War Diary	Winnezeele	25/04/1915	26/04/1915
War Diary	Vlamertinghe	27/04/1915	30/04/1915
War Diary	Steenvoorde	01/05/1915	03/05/1915
War Diary	Vlamertinghe	03/05/1915	04/05/1915
War Diary	Houtkerque	05/05/1915	07/05/1915
War Diary	Hazebrouck	08/05/1915	09/05/1915
War Diary	Ypres	10/05/1915	15/05/1915
War Diary	Reninghelst	16/05/1915	21/05/1915
War Diary	Hazebrouck	22/05/1915	23/05/1915
War Diary	Renescure	24/05/1915	29/05/1915
War Diary	Vlamertinghe	29/05/1915	30/05/1915
War Diary	Ypres	31/05/1915	31/05/1915
Heading	3rd Cavalry Division June 1915 3rd Signal Sqdn Re Vol VI		
War Diary	Ypres	01/06/1915	06/06/1915
War Diary	Renescure	07/06/1915	30/06/1915
Heading	3rd Signal Squadron July 1915		
War Diary	Renescure	01/07/1915	13/07/1915
War Diary	Pihem	14/07/1915	30/07/1915

Heading	3rd Cavalry Divisional 3rd Signal Squadron R.E Vol VIII August 15		
War Diary	Pihem	02/08/1915	06/08/1915
War Diary	Dennebroeucq	06/08/1915	30/08/1915
Diagram etc	Circuit Diagram		
Heading	3rd Signal Squadron R.E. Vol VIII Sept 1915		
War Diary	Dennebroeucq	01/09/1915	21/09/1915
War Diary	Labuissiere	22/09/1915	25/09/1915
War Diary	Mazingarbe	25/09/1915	26/09/1915
War Diary	Loos	27/09/1915	28/09/1915
War Diary	Labuissiere	29/09/1915	30/09/1915
Diagram etc	Circuit Diagram		
Heading	3rd Cavalry Division 3rd Signal Squadron R.E. Oct 15 Vol IX		
War Diary	Labuissiere	01/10/1915	03/10/1915
War Diary	Ecquedecques	04/10/1915	11/10/1915
War Diary	Bourecq	12/10/1915	19/10/1915
War Diary	Fruges	19/10/1915	31/10/1915
Diagram etc	Circuit Diagram		
Heading	3rd Cavalry Division 3 Signal Sqn Nov Vol X		
War Diary	Fruges	01/11/1915	30/11/1915
Heading	3rd Signal Sqdn Dec Vol XI		
War Diary	Fruges	01/12/1915	31/12/1915
Heading	3 Signal Sq Jan 1916 Vol XII		
War Diary	Fruges	01/01/1916	15/05/1916
War Diary	Maison-Ponthieu	15/05/1916	20/05/1916
War Diary	Fruges	21/05/1916	29/05/1916
Miscellaneous	Maison-Ponthieu		
War Diary	Fruges	01/06/1916	26/06/1916
War Diary	La Neuville	27/06/1916	05/08/1916
War Diary	Fruges	05/08/1916	24/09/1916
War Diary	Mouriez	18/10/1916	18/10/1916
War Diary	Wailly	00/11/1916	00/11/1916
War Diary	Trepied	17/12/1916	19/04/1917
War Diary	Ligescourt	01/05/1917	12/05/1917
War Diary	Beauvoir Wavans	13/05/1917	13/05/1917
War Diary	Talmas	14/05/1917	14/05/1917
War Diary	Guerrieu	15/05/1917	16/05/1917
War Diary	La Motte	17/05/1917	18/05/1917
War Diary	Flamicourt	19/05/1917	24/05/1917
War Diary	E 22 A.9.6 Villers Fancon	24/05/1917	31/05/1917
War Diary	Villers Faucon E 22 A.9.6	01/06/1917	30/06/1917
Diagram etc	Circuit Diagram		
War Diary	Villers Faucon	01/07/1917	01/07/1917
War Diary	Flamicourt	02/07/1917	04/07/1917
War Diary	Treux	05/07/1917	05/07/1917
War Diary	Doullens	06/07/1917	06/07/1917
War Diary	Sains	07/07/1917	07/07/1917
War Diary	Pernes	08/07/1917	16/07/1917
War Diary	Busnes	17/07/1917	17/10/1917
War Diary	Pernes	18/10/1917	24/10/1917
War Diary	Domart	25/10/1917	07/11/1917
War Diary	Suzanne	18/11/1917	30/11/1917
War Diary	Corbie	01/12/1917	22/12/1917
War Diary	Bouvincourt	23/12/1917	29/01/1918
War Diary	Monchy Legache	30/01/1918	12/03/1918

War Diary	Athies	13/03/1918	20/03/1918
War Diary	Beaumont Sur Beine	21/03/1918	21/03/1918
War Diary	Varesnes	22/03/1918	24/03/1918
War Diary	Muirancourt	26/03/1918	26/03/1918
War Diary	Lagny	25/03/1918	25/03/1918
War Diary	Dives	26/03/1918	26/03/1918
War Diary	Thierscourt	26/03/1918	26/03/1918
War Diary	Choisy Au Bac	27/03/1918	28/03/1918
War Diary	Le Mesnil	29/03/1918	29/03/1918
War Diary	Spons En Amienois	30/03/1918	31/03/1918
Diagram etc	Circuit Diagram		
Heading	3rd Signal Squadron, R.E. April 1918		
War Diary	Chau Brandt Boves	01/04/1918	01/04/1918
War Diary	Blangy Trouville	02/04/1918	03/04/1918
War Diary	Fouilloy	04/04/1918	04/04/1918
War Diary	Blangy Trouville	05/04/1918	05/04/1918
War Diary	Rivery	06/04/1918	10/04/1918
War Diary	Auxi Le Chateau	11/04/1918	11/04/1918
War Diary	St Pol Pernes	12/04/1918	30/04/1918
Heading	Appendices A.B.C. D and E.		
Diagram etc	Circuit Diagram of Communications Appendix A		
Diagram etc	Circuit Diagram 3rd Signal Squadron Appendix B		
Diagram etc	Circuit Diagram of Communications Appendix C		
Diagram etc	Circuit Diagram 3rd Signal Squadron Appendix D		
Diagram etc	Circuit Diagram 3rd Signal Squadron Appendix E		
War Diary	Pernes	01/05/1918	03/05/1918
War Diary	Wail	04/05/1918	04/05/1918
War Diary	Yvrench	05/05/1918	05/05/1918
War Diary	Contay	06/05/1918	31/05/1918
Diagram etc	Circuit Diagram-3rd Signal Squadron Appendix I		
Diagram etc	3rd Signal Squadron Appendix 2		
Diagram etc	Circuit Diagram of Communications Appendix 3		
Diagram etc	Circuit Diagram 3rd Signal Sqdn Appendix 4		
War Diary	Yzeux	01/06/1918	30/06/1918
Diagram etc	Circuit Diagram 3rd Signal Squadron RE 22.6.18 Appendix 1		
Diagram etc	Circuit Diagram 3rd Signal Squadron RE Appendix II		
War Diary	Yzeux	01/07/1918	31/07/1918
Diagram etc	Communication 3rd Cavalry Division July 31st 1918		
War Diary	Yzeux	01/08/1918	10/08/1918
War Diary	Boves	11/08/1918	12/08/1918
War Diary	Sains En Amienois	13/08/1918	14/08/1918
War Diary	Yzeux	15/08/1918	31/08/1918
Diagram etc	Appendix I		
Diagram etc	Appendix II		
Diagram etc	Appendix III		
Diagram etc	Appendix IV		
War Diary	Fontaine L'Etalon	01/09/1918	31/09/1918
War Diary	Poeuilly	01/10/1918	08/10/1918
War Diary	Magny-la-fosse Estrees	08/10/1918	08/10/1918
War Diary	Magny la fosse	09/10/1918	10/10/1918
War Diary	Poeuilly	04/10/1918	08/10/1918
War Diary	Magny-la-fosse Estrees	08/10/1918	08/10/1918
War Diary	Magny-la-fosse	09/10/1918	10/10/1918
War Diary	Troisvilles	10/10/1918	13/10/1918
War Diary	Elincourt	13/10/1918	13/10/1918

War Diary	Hennois Wood	14/10/1918	15/10/1918
War Diary	Troisvilles	11/10/1918	13/10/1918
War Diary	Elincourt	13/10/1918	13/10/1918
War Diary	Hennois Wood	14/10/1918	15/10/1918
War Diary	Hennois Wood	01/11/1918	06/11/1918
War Diary	Sainghain	07/11/1918	11/11/1918
War Diary	Tourpes	11/11/1918	11/11/1918
War Diary	Antoing	12/11/1918	16/11/1918
War Diary	Bassilly	17/11/1918	17/11/1918
War Diary	Enghien	18/11/1918	20/11/1918
War Diary	Waterloo	21/11/1918	21/11/1918
War Diary	Perwez	22/11/1918	22/11/1918
War Diary	Maleve	01/12/1918	14/12/1918
War Diary	Waret-L'Eveque	15/12/1918	15/12/1918
War Diary	Tinlot	16/12/1918	28/02/1919
Miscellaneous	Headquarters 7th Cavalry Brigade		
War Diary	Tinlot	01/03/1919	31/03/1919

WO 95/1146

(4)

3 Cavalry Division
Divisional Troops.

Signal Squadron

Sept 1914 - March 1919.

1914-1919
3RD CAVALRY DIVISION

3RD SIGNAL SQUADRON R.E.

SEP 1914 - MAR 1919

Confidential

War Diary

of

the 3rd Signal Squadron R.E.

3rd Cav Div.

From Sept 12th 1914 to Dec 31st 1914.

to

Mar 1919

3rd Signal Squadron R.E.

War Diary.

The 3rd Signal Squadron R.E. was formed at Ludgershall Camp, Wilts on Sept 12th 1914 with the following personnel:-

Major Atkins Gamble R.E. — Comdg.
Lieut J. Nethersole 25th I. Cav.
Lieut E.C. Braddyll 10th Lancers I. Cav.
Rejoined 2nd Lieut B. Howorth R.E. Special Reserve.
Reserve Signal Coy early 70 N.C.Os & men from the Training Depot R.E. Aldershot and the Reserve work. Signal Company.

There were no trained Pioneers or Signallers available, so Drivers who had just completed their course of Riding and Driving Drill were posted to the unit for training as Despatch Riders and semaphore signallers.
Five trained N.C.Os with signalling certificates and 3 N.C.Os from the Fortress Roster (tradesmen) were also posted.
The Unit was at first called the 2nd Signal Sqdn, but in view of the fact

that a 2nd Cav Divn & a 2nd Signal Sqdn were being formed in France; the designation of the Division being formed at Ludgershall was altered to the 3rd Cav Divn & the Sqdn was called the 3rd Signal Sqdn about the end of September.

The training of the unit proceeded steadily. Horses arrived gradually up to the establishment of 38. By Sept 29th the definite Establishment of the Unit was received from War Office and two days later the AF G 1098 - Mob Store Table, with definite authority for the issue of stores arrived.

The 29 Bicycles for the unit & most of the stores not already in possession were drawn on the 3rd & 4th Oct from the Special A.O. Depot at Portsmouth and the last two wagons arrived on Monday the 5th Oct.

At 11.15pm Oct 5th, the Unit received orders to entrain at 4.30 am the following day, and the Unit left Ludgershall accordingly at the War Establishment laid down as follows:

A H Grubb
Maj R.E.

War Establishment.   including a Vet officer and
- 5 Officers ~~a interpreter~~.
- 5 Staff Sergt Serjts
- 56 Other Ranks.
- 14 Motor Cyclist Corporals.
- 29 Riding) Horses
- 9 Draught)
- 29 Bicycles
- 14 Motor Cycles
- 3 Wagons
- 1 Water Cart
- 1 Car (Sunbeam)
- 1 Lorry (Daimler)

October 6th
The unit reached Southampton and embarked during the forenoon in S.S. MINNESOTA.

This vessel had also on board 'K' Battery R.H.A. and H.Qrs A.S.C. — the whole was under the command of Major Swaby A.S.C.

October 7th & 8th
The ship started at 4 a.m., passed DOVER at 5.30 pm and anchored off OSTEND by 4 am on the 8th. Units disembarked during the afternoon and by 8.30 pm bivouaced on the Race Course at OSTEND.
The reception of the British Soldiers

by the inhabitants of OSTEND was very hearty.

October 9th
Marched at 9.a.m to BRUGES and billeted opposite the Hotel du Commerce where Maj Gen Byng established his H'Qrs and the Signal office.
News received of the fall of ANTWERP and the evacuation of the place by the Brigade of Marines sent to it.

Oct 10th
Unit moved with the Divisional H'Qrs to OOSTCAMP and billeted.

Oct 11th to THOUROUT.
Oct 12th to ROULERS.
Oct 13th Marched via MOORSLEDE to YPRES and after leaving communication post marched to ISEGHEM and billeted.
Oct 14th marched via YPRES to the south of KEMMEL, several brushes with the enemys patrols, obtained touch with the 2nd Cav Div.
Billeted at WYTSCHAETE.
The Division brought down and captured a Taube Monoplane which was passing

Over YPRES.

Oct 15th Thursday.
    At WYTSCHAETE.

Oct 16th To YPRES and POELCAPELLE
    To ZONNEBEKE for the night.

Oct 17th   At ZONNEBEKE, the village was
    being entrenched & held by the 22nd Inf Bgde
    of the 7th Division.

Sunday 18th   At ZONNEBEKE.
    The 3rd Cav Div had been under the
orders of Sir H. Rawlinson Comdg the 4th Corps
since landing. The remainder of the
Corps consisted of the 7th Div" & a few
Corps troops.
    Communication was maintained
between H'Drs of the Corps, the 7th Div and
the units of the 3rd Cav Div entirely by
Despatch Riders, - of which the Motor
bycilists formed the most important portion.
    The roads were good & there was but little
impediment to their movement.

Monday 19th Octr.
    Moved early to MOORSLEDE to meet the
German movement from east to west.

Arrangements were made for communicating posts on the ROULERS - MENIN ROAD but the Division was unable to advance and hold a position to the east of that road. Early in the afto, it was forced to retire from MOORSLEDE on Paschendaele, where a considerable force of the French were entrenching.

H'Qrs billeted late at the Cross Roads N.E. of ST JULIAN.

Octr 20th.

Started early (4.30 a.m.) and entrenched and occupied a position between PASCHENDAELE and WESTROOSBEKE —

The German attack was supported by considerable Artillery fire and the Divn fell back to LANGEMARCK and the line of the road to ZONNEBEKE.

Motor Cycle belonging to Corpl Hobbs was left temporarily close to the advanced trenches of the French and on their retirement it had to be abandoned.

Previous to this, several motor cycles had been repaired by S.S. Willis and Corpl Keyes with the tools in possession and by using civilian workshops and materials.

These repairs included work done

for both the 6th and 7th Signal Troops.

October 21st.
Marched at 5 a.m to HOOGE on the YPRES-MENIN Road. At noon established a communicating post at the INN 1 M. due south of YPRES, near ST ELOI.
Went to VOORMEZEELE late & billeted there and at Chateau de Guiche.

October 22nd.
An early start (7.0 am) for HOOGE to support the 7th Div. which was understood to be rather pressed, then rather south to the ZANDVOORDE — HOLEBEKE line, where the Div. occupied trenches.
H.Qrs billeted at ZILLEBEKE which was the permanent report centre — all communications were by despatch riders.

October 23rd.
Still on same defensive line — making more trenches.
H.Qrs established the daily position and movable report centre at KLEIN ZILLEBEKE.
The usual routine was for one relief, consisting of a Signal Master, 3 Motor Cyclists, 3 Push Cyclists and 3 Mounted Men to accompany the General & keep the movable report centre

in touch with the permanent Report centre.

Whenever additional communicating Posts were necessary, these were formed from this party and additional men were obtained from the Report centre.

A Signal Master with a similar relief was kept on duty at the permanent Report centre. Reliefs were changed every eight or twelve hours. A fixed detail of men formed a relief, so that the same group of men were accustomed to work together.

The 1st Corps had a great success near LANGEMARCKT and killed some 1500 Germans in one of their massed attacks.

October 24th
On the same line.
7th Div lost ground about ZONNEBEKE and GELUVELDT, they were reinforced by the 2nd Div & the line restored.
Vibrator communication established with Cav Corps

October 25th   Sunday.
Obtained some telephones from Maj. Bowman Manifold Cmdg Signals 1st Corps at YPRES & brought them back also a drum of Cable.
Issued telephones to 7th Signal Troop for

se from the trenches at ZANDVOORDE to the supports.

The unit with assistance from civilians obtained locally buried 31 horses which had been killed from 400 to 500 yds East of ZILLEBEKE by shell fire on Friday night, mostly those of the 2nd Life Guards when on the picket line.

Monday October 26th
Lieut Nethersole 25th Cavalry who had been serving with the unit since its formation, left to join the 2nd Life Guards (Major Lanways ~~Sqdr~~) as the casualties in that Regiment amongst officers had been very severe.

There was some heavy fighting & the line was driven in about ZANDVOORDE and GELUVELDT.

Oct 27th
H.Qrs out to ZANDVOORDE early as usual. The usual report centres were maintained.

Oct 28th
As yesterday.

Oct 29th
Difficulty in maintaining the telephone

line to the trenches, and also in keeping the air line through from ZILLEBEKE to the Cavalry Corps at MONT NOIR –

Shell fire did constant damage, particularly along the Railway line.

Oct 30th.

The ZANDVOORDE RIDGE was lost during the early morning after a very heavy attack where the casualties in the 2nd Life Guards 7th Cav Bgde were considerable.

Both telephones & lines reported smashed by shells & abandoned.

Moved the Telegraph office at the permanent report centre to the Gangers Hut 3/4 mile south of YPRES on the ST ELOI Road. – Communication by M.C. from it to the Report Centre.

October 31st

About 8 a.m. the billets of the H'Qrs including the Signal office at ZILLEBEKE were heavily shelled.

2nd Lieut Newhouse, S&C.S. Newell and Driver Crooke were slightly wounded and three horses of the Squadron were hit.

There was some confusion and several Bicycles were temporarily abandoned. The telephone borrowed from Maj Mansfeld was

damaged and abandoned.
Movable report centre was near KLEIN
ZILLEBEKE as usual and was then moved
to HOOGE, in response to an urgent call
from the 1st Corps.
Permanent centre was at first at the
Gangers Hut & was then moved to the forked
roads at the Y of YPRES
H.Qrs at the latter place for the night.
                                    A H Grubb
                                     Major B.L.

November 1st Sunday.
Brigades moved more to the north. H.Qrs
frequently moving. Report centre at
Y of YPRES. Moved the Telegraph office
to an Estaminet on the YPRES – DICKIEBUSH
road just south of the canal.
Horses & transport brought up to the Report
Centre for the night.
The communication with the Cavalry Corps
was by a wire on the permanent line
from MONT NOIR to YPRES. Two operators
and a lineman had been lent from the
1st Signal squadron and did very good
work throughout.

Nov 2nd.
Moveable Report centre was at a farm
½ mile E of ZILLEBEKE during most of
the day, ZILLEBEKE was shelled

almost continuously. The shelling generally was very heavy.

Nov 3rd
   As yesterday.

Nov 4th.
   The 1st Corps had moved their report centre into the House formerly occupied by H⁰Qrs of 3rd Cav Div. - About 4 p.m. this was shelled and 3 Jack Johnsons hit the house or burst within a few yards of it, killing several officers & men & wounding many others - Our signal office had been moved 3 Houses down and was not injured. H⁰Qrs and signal office moved 50 yds nearer YPRES.

Nov 5th.
   Report Centre, Tel office & moveable post as usual - This involved keeping 3 relays of about 9 men each on duty during the day. Moveable post was between Hte HALTE and HOOGE. The 6th Cav Bgde took over trenches near KLEIN ZILLEBEKE, Communication by Motor Cyclist + D.R. mounted.
H⁰Qrs billeted at the same place, signal office moved 50 yds nearer to it & YPRES.

Nov 6th

Hard fighting by 7th Cav Bgde in and around KLEIN ZILLEBEKE.

Lieut Nettersole attached to 2nd Life Guards reported to have behaved very gallantly.

The Signal office on the YPRES–DICKIEBUSH road had to be moved to the chateau in the morning, as heavy shells 13 inch were falling very close to it, – the nearest one was about 50ᵡ away & the tel lines on both sides had been cut.

H.Qrs moved to this chateau just South of the D of DICKIEBUSH BEKE (100000 map) in afternoon. and the permanent report centre was established there.

The Line was kept through to the Cav Corps, bypassing the existing permanent telephone line + the air line existing to MONT NOIR. – From Cav Corps telegrams were transmitted to your H.Qrs.

Sqdn billetted in farm 500 yds away to the North – one relief + an officer were kept at the chateau.

Nov 7th

Same arrangements for communications

Nov 8th Sunday.
Same arrangement of movable report centre by day between the HALTE and HOOGE — Communication to permanent centre by Motor Cyclist and Mtd D.R.

Nov 9th.
As yesterday.

Nov 10th.
O.C. went by car to ST OMER and after seeing the Director of Army Signals, the latter ordered 'H' Cable Section from BAILLEUL to report for duty to the Division. This Section under the Command of Lieut Grundy RE arrived at 6.30 pm. — it was practically at War Establishment with 20 miles of cable + 5 Tel operators.

Nov 11th.
A cable line was put through from the Chateau to the day Report Centre at the farm occupied by the 6th Cav Bgde and 400 yds from the HALTE on the Railway line. The line mostly made use of the permanent lines to YPRES + from the Railway Station it used the

Railway Tel. line, which needed a good deal of repair. — (4 miles)

From this farm an extension was run out to Lord Cavan's (4th Guards Bgde) H°Qrs, 1 Mile East of ZILLEBEKE.
Extension of 2¼ miles.

The weather at this time was very wet and muddy, the motor cyclists only got along with great difficulty and very slowly, so that the cable lines were specially useful.

The mounted orderlys were very constantly used. — Four were kept available at the day report centre and three at the chateau day and night.

Nov 12th.
Laid a cable line 2½ miles to the 1st Corps H°Qrs at CHATEAU DES TROIS TOURS. — 1st Corps provided an operator and instrument at their end.

Also laid out a telephone line one mile to the H°Qrs of the 6th Bgde which were now moving to a farm 1 mile West of the H°Qrs chateau.

Two Telephones Portable C were used.

Nov 13th.
  Diagram of Communications.

Rather more shelling than usual, the lines were cut by shells four times during the day and repaired.

Nov 14th.
  Communications as before -
  Lines to the east of YPRES cut several times by shell fire, particularly Lord Cavan's line.
  Lieut C. G. Y Skipwith 17th Cavalry joined the squadron with one Batman and 3 horses.

Nov 15th Sunday.
Dug outs being prepared by the 3rd Field Sqdn in the Railway Cutting 200 yds south of the HALTE.

The Tel office at the farm was moved to these dug outs and the office kept open permanently day & night, as it had been for the past two nights at the farm.

Lord Cavans line now becoming very unreliable, - it was cut 6 times, probably by shell fire each time.

Nov 16th Monday.
Line to Lord Cavan was out of action & could not be got through all day -
Line along Railway was cut twice by shell fire.

During the past few days, N.C.O.s & men not on duty had been employed in repairing the roads near the Chateau. A civilian working party of about 30 men was obtained. Bricks & briqs were carted by our R.E. Transport.

Nov 17th.
After a careful inspection of the line to Lord Cavan and after repairing all cuts, it was found that the line was still not workable, so it was decided

to abandon it and use D.Rs only.

It had been found that the line laid by the 1st Corps had also been so constantly damaged, that it had been abandoned some days previously.

The 4th Guards Bgde moved their H°Qrs this day to a house 300x West of the HALTE, or some 500x away from the H°Qrs of the 3rd Cav Div, so communication by D.R. was all that was required.

The post at the dug outs was maintained for the 24 hours as usual.

Nov 18th, and 19th.
Communications as usual to Cav Corps 1st Corps, the 6th Bgde (by telephone) and the Report centre at the dug outs.

Nov 20th.
The unit less 3 Motor Cyclists and the post at the dug outs moved at 8.0 a.m. and established a communicating Post at CHATEAU LA MOTTE, 3 Miles South East of HAZEBROUCK by 1.30 pm.

H°Qrs of the Divn were however moved into HAZEBROUCK and the General established his Head Qrs at 13 Rue du Therouanne 300x south of the Main Square.

The Signal office was placed in a

house opposite and the Sqdn. billeted in the Rue de Cassell and a Farm some 1½ miles away-

The whole Division moved this day and on the following day to billets in and around HAZEBROUCK.

Nov 21st
The billets of the Brigades and units were scattered over a very wide area - it was decided to do the whole of the communications by D.R, except to the Cavalry Corps at Château La Motte to which communication was arranged by Cable & a Vibrator office was supplied from the 1st Sig Sqdn.

Nov 22nd Sunday.
The whole of the Squadron were moved into Billets in the Rue de Cassell -
H' Cable Section was ordered to proceed to BAILLEUL and report to Capt Day, R.E. it started at 2 p.m.

Nov 23rd to 30th.
No change in the positions of the different Bgdes and HdQrs of units.
Communication by motor & push cyclist and foot orderly proved ample and

satisfactory.

Leave to England for 1 officer and two N.C.Os of the unit was approved and was very much appreciated.

The work of the whole of the N.C.Os and men of the unit during the past seven weeks has been most satisfactory and appears to have given entire satisfaction to the General & other officers to whom messages have been delivered.

I wish to place on record the particularly reliable and excellent work performed regularly and often in trying circumstances by the following N.C.Os.

Sergt Norton R.C., Corpl Wright W. and 2nd Corpl Preston as Signal masters.

Sergt R.W. Shaw, Corpl T.C. Hughes and Corpl W.B. Burdett, Corpl W. Whitehead and Corpl Hobbs W.R as Motor Cyclist Despatch Riders.

Lee Cpls J.A. Tate and J. Law as Push Cyclists

Pioneers Smith A and Kettle L as Mounted Despatch Riders

2nd Corpl Simpson as acting Q.M.S

a/Corpl E.A. Helmuth A.S.C. as Motor Car Driver
and Corpl F.O. Reyes as Motor Cyclist Artificer for excellent work in repairing rapidly numerous Motor Cycles & Bicycles.

The number of messages which had usually to be registered and dealt with daily was over 200.

No 28733 Corpl Bassett F L, Motor Cyclist was gazetted on Nov 9th as a 2nd Lieut in the Royal West Kent Regt.

No 28976 Motor Cyclist Corpl M Netherole was given a commission in the Royal Garrison Artillery — and was recommended by Gen Byng for retention with the Division as an Interpreter.

A H Gamble
Maj R.E.

On reaching HAZEBROUCK, the Division was reorganised into one of three Cavalry Brigades as under:-

6th Cavalry Brigade — B.Gen D.G.M. Campbell

    3rd Dragoon Gds — Col Smith-Bingham

    1st Royal Dragoons — Col Steele

    North Somerset Yeomanry — Col Glynn

    6th Signal Troop — Capt Atkinson 1st R.G.
A.Ech. 6th Cav Field Ambulance — Maj Nicholson. V.C.

7th Cavalry Brigade — B.Gen C.T.McM. Kavanagh

    1st Life Guards — Maj. Hon A. Stanley.

    2nd Life Guards — Maj Torrie

    Leicestershire Yeomanry — Col Freake.

    7th Signal Troop — Lieut Drake 11th Hussars.
A.Ech. 7th Cav Field Amb. — Maj Herrick. RAMC.

Organization cont'd.

8th Cavalry Bgde. — B.Gen C.B. Bulkeley-Johnson

   Royal Horse Guards. — Maj Lord Tweedmouth D.S.O.

   10th Hussars — Maj Shearman

   Essex Yeomanry — Col Deacon.

   8th Signal Troop — Capt Hardy

A.Pch. 8th Cav Field Amb.

Divisional Artillery.
- I Battery R.H.A. — Maj Lamont RHA
- K. Battery R.H.A. — Maj G. White RHA
- G. Battery R.H.A. — Maj Dawson RHA
- XVth Bgde RHA. Amm Col. — Capt Walsh.
- 3rd Field Sqdn R.E. — Lieut J.C. Bowles R.E.
- 3rd Signal Sqdn — Maj Hw Grubb R.E.

H'Qrs 3rd Cav Div A.S.C. — Lt Col W.S. Swabey.

Divl Vet y units.
  13th Mobile Vet Sectn
  14th   " " "

Attached. — 3rd Cav Ammunition Park
L of C. units — 3rd Cav Supply Col.

Decr 1st 1914.

A telephone line was laid to LE TIR ANGLAIS from the Signal office, by Teeing in from the line in use to the Cavalry Corps at LA MOTTE. Two Telephones D Mk III were used - speaking was good - 4 reels of cable out.

A considerable amount of warm clothing had been obtained and was issued to the men.

Pay at 5.45 p.m.

Decr 2nd 1914.

The 3rd Cav Divn was inspected by H.M. the King. It was drawn up at 9 a.m. along the HAZEBROUCK - LA MOTTE Road.

Two Motor Cyclists with Flags were detailed to meet the King's car to the west of the town and they preceded it through the lines of horses to the chateau at La Motte.

The telephone to Le Tir Anglais was used to give the actual time of arrival of the King at HAZEBROUCK to the staff of the Divn at the Head of the Division.

The Unit paraded of the strength as under
 2 Officers
22 Mounted Men
14 Push Cyclists
 9 Motor Cyclists

the remainder were on duty at the Signal
Office and a few in billets.
Took up the Telephone line in the afternoon.

Dec 3rd and 4th.
The usual routine was continued, whilst the
Division is in reserve. N.C.Os & men not on
duty in the Signal Office were given instruction
morning and afternoon in the Portable C Telephone
and the Portable D Mark II and III and in
laying & working the D1 cable for the
telephones from the small ⅛ mile reels used
on waist belts.
The five squads take instruction in turns.

Dec 5th.
Marching order Parade 9.30 a.m. Short
route march of the whole unit. The weather was
very wet and cold with hail & sleet.

Dec 6th Sunday.
Inspection of clothing and kit — issued
a good deal of clothing and under clothing.
The N.C.Os and men are now all properly
clothed and equipped.

A.H. Gamble
Maj R.E.

Organization for Signal Office work.

The working members of the Squadron are still permanently allotted into five Reliefs or squads consisting each of

    One Signal Master. (Sergt or Corpl.)
    3 or 4 Push Cyclists
    2 or 3 Motor Cyclists
    3 or 4 Mounted Men.

Each relief comes on duty at 6 pm for a period of 24 hours.

The relief next for duty comes on duty from 6 pm to 9 pm on the day previous to its tour of duty to cope with the rush of correspondence which usually takes place then.

The mounted men are only on duty when not necessarily required to exercise, water & feed their horses.

In addition there requires always to be an Operator and lineman on duty.

The usual number at the Signal Office on duty day and night is thus eleven.

In addition there is the extra strength of men from 6 to 9 pm and the motor cyclists next for duty are kept at their billets and are constantly required for work when next for duty.

The following are the messages dealt with:

Messages dealt with.   Total

Dec 2nd   Incoming 35 } 174.
          Outgoing 139 }

Dec 3rd   Incoming 53 } 201.
          Outgoing 148 }

Dec 4th   Incoming 58 } 171
          Outgoing 113 }

Dec 5th   Incoming 87 } 186.
          Outgoing 99 }

Sunday.
Dec 6th   In   81 } 225.
          Out   144 }

Casualties during week.
Joined from Signal Depot Advanced Base Dec 2nd
7512 2/Cpl Watts W, 25368 Dr Owens W, 25433 Dr Black A, and No 3718 Pte Caps W.

No 28975 Motor Cyclist Corpl Nothersole N.B quitted on the 2nd to take up a commission as 2nd Lieut in the R.G.A.

No 15811 Dr N.Curray, admitted to Hospital on the 5th

A.H.Grubb
Maj/R.E.

Dec 7th Monday. to Dec 12th

    Daily instruction in the use of Telephones. and Trained signallers were out for two nights with lamps.

    Training with semaphore was also resumed and Mounted men were given exercises in Map reading & finding their way across country.

The following messages were dealt with:-

Date	In/Out	Total
Dec 7th	Incoming 47 / Outgoing 119	166
Dec 8th	In 36 / out 182	218
Dec 9th	In 81 / out 151	232
Dec 10th	In 48 / out 206	254
" 11th	In 73 / out 133	206
" 12th	In 84 / out 116	200

A regular post was established and "ordinary" letters were only sent out to Brigades & Divisional units three times daily - at 7.30 a.m., 12.30 pm and 6.30 pm. All letters to all officers in Hazebrouck whether urgent or ordinary were delivered at once, except that ordinary letters are not delivered between 10.30 p.m and 7.30 a.m.

Urgent messages are of course delivered at any time as soon as possible.

Casualties.
The following N.C.O & men joined from the Signal Depot Le Mans on the 12th.

No 24901 2/Cpl D Turner
    24366 Pioneer E.C Gowing
    25625   "   L Hurd
    22074 Sapper G. Sloper
    27309 Sapper W.J. Whyte
    6954   Pte   C. Earl.

On the 10th No 28996. Motor Cyclist Cpl. R. Channon joined

On the 9th.
    No 25554   Lr P. Coughlan) transferred to the
        25838   Lr G. Nairn.   ) 8th Signal Troop.

On the 11th
    No 7512 L/Cpl W Watts was admitted to Hospl.

A H Grubb
Maj R.E

Dec 13th Sunday.
   AT HAZEBROUCK. packing up and preparing to move.

Dec 14th.
   No 1 Relief started at 7.30 a.m. & proceeded to the Report Centre & the Rendez-Vous of the Division at forked roads 1½ miles NE of BAILLEUL. Report Centre moved on to near DRANOUTRE by 10.30 a.m. Communicating post left at the forked roads and immediate connection with Cavalry Corps and our permanent report centre at ST JANS CAPELLE. was established.
   Communication by Motor Cycle from both places to advanced post of Cav Corps at BAILLEUL, the 2nd Corps there and to R.C.G. (The Tel office of advanced station of G. H.Q.)
   1.30 p.m. Div H.Q. moved back to ST JANS CAPELLE and Brigades to their billets. Buzzer office established then from ST JANS CAPELLE to Cav Corps at BAILLEUL; but it was removed during after-
   Cable line was laid out by H-Cable Section (temporarily borrowed from R.C.G.) from 6th Cav Bgde at BAILLEUL. 20 Rue de Lille. to ST JANS CAPELLE and the line worked by telephone - first by

Portable Cs then by D Mark III's.

Telephone cable D1 was run out to 7th Cav Bgde at BERTHEN; but after being through temporarily at 5.30 pm, a diss- occurred.

Communication was arranged by wire to Cav Corps La Motte from R.C.G. and from 2nd Cav Bgde at BERTHEN where a Motor Cyclist was kept during the night.

Communication was also established with 5th Infantry Div, whose H°Qrs were in the vicinity.

Dec 15th

Division standing by all day in billets.

Improved lines to 6th Cav Bgde and 7th Cav Bgde which was put through & fairly satisfactory communication was established by the afternoon. Distance nearly 2 miles (10 drums) was rather much for satisfactory working of Telephone this time of year, though the line is very largely poled.

Other lines as before.

Arranged for all G.H.Q. and ordnance work to be ~~transmitted~~ sent to R.C.G. BAILLEUL for transmission.

Decr 16th

Division moved back to its former Billets in and around HAZEBROUCK.

The Signal office was established in its former place 20 Rue de Therouane.

Gen Byng still at No 13 Rue de Therouane but position of other staff offices changed.

Billets of unit also changed in a few cases + some improvements made.

Officers at 53 Rue de Cassell.

Decr 17th to 20th

Routine work as usual.

Class started in morse signalling with Flags and trained signallers were exercised in lamp work.

Casualties

Dec 18th Pte René Poendein 31st Dragoons joined as Interpreter. with one horse.

The following messages were dealt with:-

Sunday – Dec 13th — Incoming 62, Outgoing 156 } 218

ST JANS CAPELLE.
Dec 14th — In 31, Out 80 } 111

Dec 15th — In 51, Out 144 } 195

HAZEBROUCK
Dec 16th — In 76, Out 98 } 174

Dec 17th — In 129, Out 152 } 281

Dec 18th — In 90, Out 168 } 258

Dec 19th — In 133, Out 213 } 346.

A H Grubb
Maj R.E.

Sunday Dec 20th

Orders were issued again permitting leave of absence to be granted to 25% of the officers and N.C.O of the Divisional Units for 72 hours and this was subsequently extended to permit of a weeks leave being granted.

Lieut C. Skipwith 17th Cavalry proceeded by the 8.53 pm train on 6 clear days leave and Sergt James on 5 days Xmas leave.

Dec 21st

Training with semaphore & Morse. Lamp signalling with trained signallers 4.30pm to 7pm. 4 stations out.

22nd

O.C. went in to St Omer and obtained a light G.W.K. Car 6-8 horse power for trial, to ascertain whether it was suitable for use carrying despatches & parcels when Motor cycles could not run.

Car issued by the Director of Army Signals Driver Channon Motor cyclist placed in charge.

Scheme of Night signalling with the 8th Signal Troop was carried out.

23rd/24th - Training as usual.

Dec 25th Christmas Day.
At 10.30 pm, the unit paraded and gave three hearty cheers for the King & Queen. Their Majesties Christmas Cards were presented to every man individually.

The Christmas Gift from the Princess Mary was presented to each man individually at 5.30 pm. The N.C.O. & men very much appreciated receiving the cards & gifts.

Dec 26th. Training as usual.
Laid out one mile of the new enamelled telephone wire and reeled it up again.
Also laid out two miles of D5 cable from the Line & S. wagon & left the line out.

Casualties during week.
Sqdn Sgt Maj A.C. Litley was admitted to Hospital on the 23rd.
On the 23rd No 12506 Sgt Norton was appointed Actg Sqn Q.M.S. vice S.Q.M.S. Simpson admitted to Hospital in October.
No 3718 Pte Capps W. 15th Hussars was appointed Lce Cpl (unpaid)

On 24th 2nd Cpl Preston was appointed Actg Sgt. vice Sergt Norton.

The following messages were dealt with at the Signal Office.

HAZEBROUCK.

Day		In/Out	Count	Total	Urgent
Sunday Dec 20th		Incoming	135	266	Includes urgent messages
		Outgoing	131		
Monday 21st		In	134	219	—
		Out	85		
Tues. 22nd		In	109	352	—
		Out	243		
Wed. 23rd		In	115	297	8
		Out	182		
Th 24th		In	110	245	11
		Out	135		
Christmas Day		In	43	122	—
		Out	79		
Sat 26th		In	90	271	4
		Out	181		

A.H. Grubb
Maj R.E.

HAZEBROUCK. 37

Monday Dec 28th to Thursday 31st.

Unit laid down and maintained a line of enamelled telephone wire 2½ miles long. A Report on the trial was submitted to the Director of Army Signals on 1-1-15.

As compared with D1 cable, the wire is much lighter, is rather more easily laid & gives good insulation resistance when new.

It breaks very easily, is difficult to examine & maintain & cannot easily be reeled up.

A line 2½ miles long of D5 cable was laid & maintained for practice.

During this week two men were allowed to leave to England for periods of 72 hours each.

N.C.Os were granted 96 hours leave.

The weather was at first frosty, then very wet.

The reliefs on duty at the Signal office were mounted at 9 a.m. & remained on duty until the following day at 9 a.m.

Casualties: Nil.

38

The following messages were dealt with at the Signal office.

					urgent
Sunday Dec 27th	Incoming	109	}	239	8
	Outgoing	130			
Mon 28th	In	100	}	238	2
	Out	138			
Tues 29th	In	171	}	305	5
	Out	134			
Wed 30th	In	112	}	262	15
	Out	150			
Thurs 31st	In	113	}	236	18
	Out	123			

A H Gamble
Maj R.E.
O.C. 3rd Signal Sqdn R.E.
2-1-15.

WAR DIARIES

OF

3RD SIGNAL SQDRN. R.E.

3RD CAVALRY DIVISION

FOR

JANUARY – DECEMBER

1915.

Jan. 1915.

121/4194

3rd Signal Squadron RE.

Vol III. 1 — 31.1.15.

Confidential.

War Diary of the 3rd Signal Squadron, R.E.

3rd Cavalry Division.

From January 1st to 31st 1915.

A Fitzgerald
Major R.E.
2-2-15.

January 1915.
Sheet 1.

Instructions regarding War Diaries and Intelligence
Summaries are contained in F.S. Regs., Part II.
and the Staff Manual respectively. Title pages
will be prepared in manuscript.

WAR DIARY of 3rd Signal Squadron of Army Form C. 2118.
INTELLIGENCE SUMMARY 3rd Cavalry Division.
(Erase heading not required.)

Hour, Date, Place	Summary of Events and Information	Remarks and references to Appendices
January 1st Friday. HAZEBROUCK.	The unit is in billets at HAZEBROUCK, whilst the 3rd Cav Div is being held in reserve. Training is carried out daily for all N.C.Os. & men not actually employed in routine work of the Signal Office & other Signal duties in the Division. Morse with flag & lamp signalling is practised to a two times weekly, but not time except in practising laying Telegraph & Telephone lines with D5, D1, and the new "Cable" supplied on Dec 24th 1914. The unit is divided into 5 reliefs of 10 or 11 men each excluding a Senior NCO as Signal Master, mounted men cyclists and motor cyclists. Be aground put 1½ miles of enamelled wire line through, a second look at its estimation of D1 cable replaced if by enamelled wire. There were so many leaks that the line was not strong k/m. 12-3¾ miles until 12.15 p.m.	
Jan 2nd	Raining all day. Horses exercised. Messages dealt with:-	outgoing - ingoing - incoming Total. Jan 1st 153 100 253 " 2nd 161 106 267

Sheet 2.

WAR DIARY of 3rd Signal Sqdn F.F.
or
~~INTELLIGENCE SUMMARY~~

Army Form C. 2118.

(Erase heading not required.)

Hour, Date, Place	Summary of Events and Information	Remarks and references to Appendices
Jan 3rd Sunday.	— Voluntary Church Service. No 13 Rue de Cassel.	
Jan 4th. HAZEBROUCK.	Rained – Indoor instruction in morning. Lamp Signalling 4.30 p.m. New electric signalling lamps used – After some adjustment it was made to work satisfactorily.	
Jan 5th	Reeled up line of D5 cable which had been maintained for practice since Dec 28th. Left an N.C.O. to give instruction to 7th Signal Troop in laying telephone lines.	
Jan 6th	Reeled up the enamelled wire which had been out since Dec 28th. The wire was much chafen and damaged. Raining nearly all day.	
Jan 7th & H.	Raining in morning. Laid one mile of wire enamelled on ground under water in the canal to the banks for test – Very faint signals obtained on the Fuller 7th D III Telephone as speaking. Poled a portion of the line with poles 15" to 20 yds bearing. Strong gale blowing train was constantly breaking. No poles were raised.	
" 9th.	Squadron paraded in marching order, wagons fully packed from starting mark – Rained heavily until midday. Paed enamelled wire + D III Tel delivered to 7th S.T. Recd wire 5.30pm	

Sheet 3.

WAR DIARY 3rd Signal Sqdn R.E.
INTELLIGENCE SUMMARY
(Erase heading not required.)

Army Form C. 2118.

Hour, Date, Place	Summary of Events and Information	Remarks and references to Appendices

Casualties during week 3rd to 9th.
Joined Unit:
on the 8th. No 29524 Sapper Tanwell W. Trade. Telegraphist officer.
     "   29536   "   Michel C.
     "   29538   "   Southcott P.
     "   29573   "   King W.

The following number of messages were dealt with:-

	outgoing	urgent	Incoming	Total
(Sunday) Jan 3rd.	108	—	119	227
Jan 4th.	135	(11)	73	208
" 5th	159	(21)	67	226
" 6th	211	(5)	80	291
" 7th	159	(4)	112	271
" 8th	80	(4)	75	155
" 9th	79	(5)	146	225

There were no changes in the diagram of communication. viz: Lui (Vitalion office) to Cavalry Corps LA MOTTE. L. Roto (6th Brigade. LES LAURIERS - (on the LA MOTTE - MERVILLE Road) - 7th Bgde. Chateau at HONDEGHEM and 8th Bgde - in HAZEBROUCK.

Ottoguth
Maj. R.E.

Sheet 4

January 1915.

WAR DIARY
or
INTELLIGENCE SUMMARY
(Erase heading not required.)

3rd Signal Sqdn FT   Army Form C. 2118.

Instructions regarding War Diaries and Intelligence Summaries are contained in F.S. Regs., Part II. and the Staff Manual respectively. Title pages will be prepared in manuscript.

Hour, Date, Place	Summary of Events and Information	Remarks and references to Appendices

Jan 10th HAZEBROUCK. Divine Service (C.of E.) at 10 a.m. —
One Telephone D III issued to 6th Signal Troop & another to 8th Signal Troop.

Jan 11th. Extended enamelled air line to two miles – repaired it in several places and put in 21 poles. Faint signals only over the 2 miles.
5 – 7 p.m. Lamp Signalling.
A second horse transferred to Lieut. J.N. Cooper A.V.C.

Jan 12th. Put the enamelled wire line through – The enamel of the line in the water had become very soft and was easily scraped off by the finger nail. Reel of rotten J line in water.
Class in Morse Flag this evening at Buzzer.

Jan 13th & 14th Class with Flag & Buzzer. Instruct. days.

Jan 15th. Practice Divisional Scheme: Divisional HQrs just north of HAZEBROUCK. – Telephone line laid to 6th Bgde at LA KREULE. (D I cable). Cable Line D5 with ⅔ improved Cable Cart to the Lotenniet du Coq, ¾ mile on the HONDEGHEM Road, and a D IV enamelled wire line to farm 400 x W. of preceding established for the 8th Bgde. – Lines through by 1 p.m. In the afternoon squads returned air enamelled wire & improved cork & faults were found

Sheet 5.

Army Form C. 2118.

WAR DIARY
or
INTELLIGENCE SUMMARY
(Erase heading not required.)

Instructions regarding War Diaries and Intelligence Summaries are contained in F.S. Regs., Part II. and the Staff Manual respectively. Title pages will be prepared in manuscript.

Hour, Date, Place	Summary of Events and Information	Remarks and references to Appendices
HAZEBROUCK Jan 16th	Lines laid preceding day were rested up. 2 officers and 17 men inoculated against Enteric Fever. Casualties during week:- No 28746 Motor Cyclist Corpl Boyle was granted an extension of leave of absence in England by the Col'c R.E. Records on medical certificate and he was transferred to the Reserve Signal company at Aldershot. The following messages were dealt with:- Incoming. Outgoing - (Expt). Total. Jan 10th 76 204 (12) 280 " 11th 75 164 (13) 239 " 12th 80 138 - 218 " 13th 98 81 (4) 179 " 14th 91 135 (3) 226 " 15th 63 137 (8) 200 " 16th 102 152 (4) 254.	A.W.Griffiths Major R.E.

Sheet 6.

WAR DIARY 3rd Signal Sqdn. F.F.
or
INTELLIGENCE SUMMARY

Army Form C. 2118.

(Erase heading not required.)

Hour, Date, Place	Summary of Events and Information	Remarks and references to Appendices
Jan 17th HAZEBROUCK. Jan 18th Jan 19th	Divine Service by the Rev. A.T. Hill at 6.30 p.m. 13 Rue de Cassel. Overhauling stores. Practice Divisional Signal Scheme in conjunction with the 3 Signal Troops of the Brigades. General Idea – The Division is holding an entrenched position facing north from the point H of HONDEGHEM to LA BREARDE (exclusive). The Squadron laid out the lines as under: H'Qrs – ½ mile N of the level (A) to 6th H.sq'ds at farm 400× N.W. of LA NREULE crossing at HAZEBROUCK (B) to 7th H.sq'd at houses 500× S of the brooks crossing the HAZEBROUCK – HONDEGHEM Road. (C) to 8th H.sq'd at farm where the brook crosses the MERE MELIN – HONDEGHEM Road. Signal troops each laid out telephone lines to the line of trenches assumed the about the LONGUECROIX – LABREADE Road. Communications were through by 11.30 a.m. A line was D1+ enamelled wire with Portable telephone. B line was with D5 cable + vibrator. C line was with D1+ enamelled wire with D III telephone.	
Jan 20th " 21st " 23rd	Re-established communication over the above three lines. Wet day – overhauling stores. Morse Signalling Drill inspection. 10 officers attended Brigade Scheme of VI H.sq'd.	Two officers attended Brigade scheme with VII H.sq'd. 1 officer and 15 men inoculated. O H Spirit Major

Sheet 7

WAR DIARY 3rd Signal Squadron **Army Form C. 2118.**
or
INTELLIGENCE SUMMARY
(Erase heading not required.)

Hour, Date, Place	Summary of Events and Information	Remarks and references to Appendices
Week Jan 17th–23rd.	Casualties:- No. 25341 L/Cpl Hemming — In Hospital 18th to 20th. No. 12506 Cpl. (now actg S.S.M.) R. Norton. Gte Seyrant-dte Col 30-12-14 Promotion No 10747, 10758 & 10759. No. 22150 2nd/Cpl. (now actg Sergt.) F. Breslin to be corporal dated 8-11-14 20th Two office telegraphist Cpls while and Sapper Joy sent by 1st. Promotion No as above. Cav. Corps Signal Sqdn rejoined their own unit. The following messages were dealt with:- Incoming Outgoing (input) Total Sunday Jan 17th 61 102 163 Jan 18th 110 200 (7) 310 " 19th 58 116 (4) 174 " 20th 32 170 (11) 202 " 21st 50 128 178 " 22nd 74 80 154 " 23rd 90 217 (5) 307	Okegado Major.

Sheet 78.

WAR DIARY 3rd Signal Sqdn

or

INTELLIGENCE SUMMARY

(Erase heading not required.)

Army Form C. 2118.

Instructions regarding War Diaries and Intelligence Summaries are contained in F. S. Regs., Part II. and the Staff Manual respectively. Title pages will be prepared in manuscript.

Hour, Date, Place	Summary of Events and Information	Remarks and references to Appendices
Jan 24th HAZEBROUCK. Jan 25th	Sunday. Flag Signalling &schemes of D.R. with mounted men across country. It was decided to reduce the establishment of the Squadron to that recently issued from a War office for a Cavalry Division Signal Sqdn — though the establishment had not be actually received in the Division. The New Establishment is as under.	

Detail	Officers	Staff/Sgts	Sgts	Unclassed	Rank & file	Total	Horses R	Horses D	Horses Total	Bicycles	Motor cycles
Captain	1	.	.	.	.	1	.	.	.	.	.
Subalterns	2	.	.	.	.	2	.	.	.	.	.
Sqdn Serjt Maj	.	1	.	.	.	1	.	.	.	.	.
Serjeants	.	.	1	.	.	1	4	.	4	.	.
S & C. Smith	.	.	1	.	1	2	1	.	1	.	.
Corporal	.	.	.	.	1	1	1	.	1	.	.
2nd Corpl	.	.	.	.	13	13	6	.	6	9	.
Sapper	.	.	.	1	4	4	.	6	6	1	.
Drivers	.	.	.	.	6	6	6	6	.	3	.
Batmen	.	.	.	2	9	12	.	.	.	.	12
Motor cyclists	.	.	1	.	.	.	.	.	.	.	.
Total Sqdn	3	3	3	3	34	43	15	6	21	13	12
Driver A.S.C. (Att)	.	.	.	2	2	.	.	.	.	.	.
Total	3	3	3	36	45	15	6	21	13	12

* Reinforcement to bring up to bases — Corpl (signaller) and 4 men.

Abergwili Neyre

Sheet 9.

WAR DIARY of 3rd Signal Sqdn V.2.
or
INTELLIGENCE SUMMARY
(Erase heading not required.)

Army Form C. 2118.

Instructions regarding War Diaries and Intelligence Summaries are contained in F.S. Regs., Part II. and the Staff Manual respectively. Title pages will be prepared in manuscript.

Hour, Date, Place	Summary of Events and Information	Remarks and references to Appendices
	Establishment of a Cavalry Division Signal Squadron cont:-	Establishment issued from War office S.D.2 dated 14-12-14.
	Transport - Motor Cars (small) 2 - Wagon Lumbered S. 1. -	
	Detail of Trades -	
	Shoeing and Carriage Smith 1 Telegraphists { Field line 4 { office 6 Signallers 6 Motor Cyclist Artificers 2 Motor Cyclists 10 Drivers and Batmen 10 —— 39	
HAZEBROUCK Jan 25th	cont:- The G.W.R. small car issued by the Director of Army Signals on Dec 22nd for trial was returned to the Director of Transport of G.H.Q. (St Omer) - and a report submitted to LAS saying that the car was considered the unsuitable for use in its service as a despatch Riding Car.:- In its place a 8-10 HP Singer car was obtained for the establishment of the unit. As the Transport of the unit was appreciated as quite inadequate, the D.D.T. approved of the lorry now with the unit being retained temporarily. A. Hozgoulf majre.	

Sheet 10

WAR DIARY
or
INTELLIGENCE SUMMARY
(Erase heading not required.)

Army Form C. 2118.

Hour, Date, Place	Summary of Events and Information	Remarks and references to Appendices
HAZEBROUCK. Jan 26th	Mounted men practised in Cross Country work.	
Jan 27th	Squadron Saddled up at 9 am & wagons packed ready to move at a moment's Notice. Squadron paraded at 10.40 am (Strength 50 all ranks) for inspection at 11.30 am by Field Marshal Sir J. French. The Field Sqdn, the Signal Sqdn and the R.A.M.C. of the Division were drawn up in a hollow square, — after the inspection, the F.M. addressed the unit & congratulated the unit on the excellent work performed. He spoke of the several cheery notes by the Royal Engineers and of how the Corps were clearly holding fresh lustre to their already brilliant achievements. The following 10 horses were transferred to the units as under:— Sqdn. No. 4, 22, 23, 34, 21 — to the Leicester Yeomanry. No 20 — to H.Q. 6th Cav Bgde No 9 & 36 — to 3rd Field Sqdn No 12 & 27 — to G. Battery R.H.A.	
Jan 28th	On reduction of strength, the Squadron was reorganized into three reliefs of about 12 men each, each relief containing Cyclists mounted men & motor cyclists. The reliefs are under Sergt Preston, Corpl Wright and Sergt James respectively. The drivers & officers batmen are not included in reliefs. The following N.C.Os and men — whose names had previously been submitted	A. H. Grould Maj. R.E.

Sheet 11

WAR DIARY
or
INTELLIGENCE SUMMARY

Army Form C. 2118.

(Erase heading not required.)

Hour, Date, Place	Summary of Events and Information	Remarks and references to Appendices
Jan 28th cont.	to the O.C. Signal Depot Abbeville, were despatched by the afternoon train to the Signal Depot. No 20658 Corpl Hughes S, 25341 Sergt Hemmings H, No 25422 Sergt Smith A. 26000 Sr Adams A 25433 Sr Black A 25585 Sr Carey P. 26103 Sr Coff A. 24826 Sr Calder C. 24879 Sr Bates W. 26117 Sr Gilpin J. 25478 Sr Storie F. 17366 Sr Hussey F. 24738 Sr Lyne W 25649 Sr Owens J. 24985 Sr Prescott F. The Unit laid two lines of cable each 2¾ miles long abating 4.45 p.m. work was completed thus though by 9 p.m. Lines were tested - men returned to billets 10 p.m.	
Jan 29th	There were no breaks in either line in the morning, the lines were improved throughout later in the day the line was rested up. Pay at 6 p.m.	
Jan 30th	The second line was rested up. Arrangements made for the move of the Signal Office to 76 Rue de MERVILLE,	
Sunday. Jan 31st	The Signal Office was moved & a cablelin in extension run from the old office to the new one.	Oh Sheriff Major R.E.

Sheet 12.

WAR DIARY
or
INTELLIGENCE SUMMARY

Army Form C. 2118.

Hour, Date, Place	Summary of Events and Information	Remarks and references to Appendices
HAZEBROUCK.	The following jubilee casualties occurred during week 24th to 31st. Transfers.	
25th Jan	No 25093 Sr Hall W. No 23529 Sr Murphy H. transferred to 8th Signal Troop.	
26th Jan	No 25991 Sr Hook A. transferred to the 7th Signal Troop.	
31st Jan	No 14101 Farr Sergt Mickleborough - transferred to Cav Corps Sig Sqdn.	
31st Jan	25554 Sr Coughlan P., 25838 Sr Nairn G. transferred from 8th Sig Tp to Sqdn.	

The following messages were dealt with.

	Incoming	Outgoing	W.	Total.
Jan 24th	70	98	(7)	168
" 25th	77	129	(13)	206
" 26th	77	174	(18)	251
" 27th	75	142	(7)	217
" 28th	130	185	(17)	315
" 29th	97	139	-	236
" 30th	111	140	(12)	251
" 31st	133	153	(10)	286

Note Transmitted messages are only counted once in the above figures tic all previous numbers of messages given.

A Westgarth
Major.

Sheet 13.

WAR DIARY
or
INTELLIGENCE SUMMARY
(Erase heading not required.)

Army Form C. 2118.

Hour, Date, Place	Summary of Events and Information	Remarks and references to Appendices
Jan 1915.	Signal office arrangements. The diagram & arrangements for communication remained practically unchanged throughout the month. The line built/to wireless office) to the Cavalry Corps at LA MOTTE was maintained. This line was permanent one, passing through the central telegraph office HAZEBROUCK, hence if could be tested – and where telegraph communication to 3rd army could be obtained. D.R. Communication was carried out to the 6th B'gde at LES LAURIERS, on the MERVILLE Road, the 7th B'gde at the CHATEAU HONDEGHEM, and the 8th B'gde in HAZEBROUCK by regular posts starting at 7.30 a.m., 12.30 p.m. & 6.30 p.m. and by urgent messages as required. – Messages for ordnance at the Base were handed in to the 3rd Army for despatch & also sealed communications for G.H.Q. which was sent in lines daily by Motor Cyclist. On the 28th inst. H'Qrs of the 6th Cav B'gde moved to THIENNES – Corner House on the Square and H'Qrs 8th Cav B'gde to the chateau 3/4 mile E. of EBBLINGHEM on the EBBLINGHEM – HAZEBROUCK Road. Other units to which despatch riders are delivered are located as under:– 3rd Field Sqdn R.E. – House ½ mile N.W of HAZEBROUCK STATION on the HONDEGHEM Road. Ammunition Col. – ST SYLVESTRE CAPPEL – Ammunition Park – white chateau 200x N of MORBECQUE. Supply Column – Café du Gare MORBECQUE. H'Qrs A.S.C. – Farm 500x S.E. of level crossing on the LA MOTTE Road.	

Sheet 14

WAR DIARY 3rd Signal Sqdn RE

or

~~INTELLIGENCE SUMMARY~~

(Erase heading not required.)

Army Form C. 2118.

Instructions regarding War Diaries and Intelligence Summaries are contained in F. S. Regs., Part II. and the Staff Manual respectively. Title pages will be prepared in manuscript.

Hour, Date, Place	Summary of Events and Information	Remarks and references to Appendices
	Signal office arrangements cont'd. Staff offices R.H.A. – 25 Rue d'Saire – A motor cyclist was permanently kept h/t RA to take messages to & from the RAH²Q'rs to Batteries (C. R. + Q.). The R.A.M.C. found their own orderlies at the Signal office. A.D.M.S. was at 35 Rue de Cassel. G,O,C's address – 11 Rue de Thérouanne. G.S. Staff – 11 Rue de MORBECQUE – A + Q staff moved on 28th to 80 Rue de MERVILLE.	
Jan 31st	It was settled that Capt FAIRCLOUGH R.H.A. was to take over command of the unit from Major A.H.W. GRUBB R.E who was to proceed to England for other duty.	Note. Feb 1st Capt Fairclough joined & took over, and on Feb 2nd Major Grubb was to proceed to 1st War office & report to A.A.G. R.E.
Feb 1st 1915.		AHSGrubb Maj R.E O.C. 3rd Signal Sqdn R.E.

FEB. 1915

3rd Cavalry Division

3rd Signal Squadron. R.E.

Vol III 1 – 28.2.15

Sheet 9

WAR DIARY of 3rd Signal Squadron
INTELLIGENCE SUMMARY

Army Form C. 2118.

(Erase heading not required.)

Instructions regarding War Diaries and Intelligence Summaries are contained in F. S. Regs., Part II. and the Staff Manual respectively. Title pages will be prepared in manuscript.

Hour, Date, Place	Summary of Events and Information	Remarks and references to Appendices

Breaches were repaired & the wire cable of Squadron troops expended was made up.
The mounted men of the unit were employed in delivering the mid-day post.
A court martial was held on Dr Barnes on the 19th inst.

The average number of messages dealt with daily from 14th – 28th Feb. was.

	Outgoing	Urgent	Incoming	Total
14th – 20th	178	9	105	283
21st – 27th	135	17	110	235

E. H. Fawthorp
Capt R.A.
Comdg 3rd Signal Squadron

A

Circuit Diagram 5th Feb

18th French Div
POTIJZE

↑ BLG
→ French
PG ZILLEBEKE RESERVE
VCR YPRES

Divnl HQ (night)
ECD POPERINGHE

VC HAZEBROUCK

ZCO LAMOTTE

After 6th Feb line PG/BLG was doubled

S. M. Fairtlough
Capt. R.A

February 1915 Sheet I

WAR DIARY of 3rd Signal Squadron

Army Form C. 2118.

Instructions regarding War Diaries and Intelligence Summaries are contained in F.S. Regs., Part II. and the Staff Manual respectively. Title pages will be prepared in manuscript.

INTELLIGENCE SUMMARY

(Erase heading not required.)

Hour, Date, Place	Summary of Events and Information	Remarks and references to Appendices
Feb 1st Monday HAZEBROUCK	Captain E.H. Fawcthorpe R.A took over command of 3rd Signal Squadron. Major Grubb D.S.O. proceeded to England.	
Feb 2nd	Lt Shipwith arranged for billets in neighbourhood of YPRES for unit. At 3 pm a party, with three motor lorries, proceeded to YPRES & ran out lines + arranged for intercommunication for the 3rd Cav Division during their stay in the trenches East of YPRES. This party of war composed of men from Cav Corps Sigs, 3rd Cav Bde Sigs & 4th Bde Sigs. On this night three lines (DS) were laid from Divl H.Q (red Chateau on YPRES—MENIN road) to (i) 4th Cav Bde H.Q (Farm just North of ZILLEKE) to (ii) Jo railway level crossing on POPERINGHE—YPRES road for one with FCO and LCO. In addition two further lines were laid from 4th Bde H.Q (i) to position of French Reserve (CAVAN'S HOUSE) (ii) 2 mile guards H.Q (mile East of Cavans House).	

1247 W 3299 200,000 (E) 8/14 J.B.C.&A. Forms C. 2118/11.

WAR DIARY of 3rd SiS Squadron
or INTELLIGENCE SUMMARY

Army Form C. 2118.

Sheet 2

Instructions regarding War Diaries and Intelligence Summaries are contained in F.S. Regs., Part II. and the Staff Manual respectively. Title pages will be prepared in manuscript.

(Erase heading not required.)

Hour, Date, Place	Summary of Events and Information	Remarks and references to Appendices
Feb 2nd (continued)	All lines of D5 cable were laid from motor lorries belonging to Cavalry Corps Signals. The party returned to HAZEBROUCK sow at 5am on morning of 3rd Feb.	
Feb 3rd	Conference of Brigade Staff Officers was held at HAZEBROUCK and after Capt Fawthrop & Lt Bradyll with 1st & 2nd reliefs proceeded by motor lorry to YPRES, Lt Skipwith remaining at HAZEBROUCK with 3rd relief to maintain communication with Brigades & Div'nal troops as formerly. Owing to shortage of operators five were lent by Cav Corps Signals. By 9pm communication was established according to attached diagram. Communication with 18th French Division (General LEFEVRE) at POTIJZE by telephone worked by French operators.	Appendix A

Sheet 3

WAR DIARY of 3rd Signal Squadron

INTELLIGENCE SUMMARY

Army Form C. 2118.

(Erase heading not required.)

Instructions regarding War Diaries and Intelligence Summaries are contained in F. S. Regs., Part II. and the Staff Manual respectively. Title pages will be prepared in manuscript.

Hour, Date, Place	Summary of Events and Information	Remarks and references to Appendices
Feb 4th YPRES	Communication was satisfactory during the day with Cav Corps & 5th Corps but the lines were to 7th Bde. were constantly cut by shell fire, to minimise this as far as possible a second line (D1) was laid during night of 4th/5th across country by 1st Bradyll to 7th Bde. H.Q. & "bridged" in four places to the original line. After this was done communication to 7th Bde did not again break down although but both lines had to be repaired nightly. The French wished us to take over the lines from 2nd Life Guards & Blues to the French Command at HOOGE this was found to be impossible as all the French instruments were magneto Bells & consequently could not be worked by D3 Klopfones. The final arrangement was that 3rd Sig Squadron gave the French two kilometres of D5 cable & that they (French) left their lines & instruments in position & these were worked by the Regimental interpreters.	

Sheet A

WAR DIARY of 3rd Signal Squadron
or
INTELLIGENCE SUMMARY

Army Form C. 2118.

(Erase heading not required.)

Hour, Date, Place	Summary of Events and Information	Remarks and references to Appendices

Feb 4th (Cont)

The General Staff returned each night to POPERINGHE. Communication was established between 124 Rue d'YPRES POPERINGHE and day report centre (Red château (YPRES-MENIN road) as follows:—

A vibrator & separator was added to the line to 5th Corps & the 5th Corps ran a line through a separator from their office in POPERINGHE to a vibrator office at 124 Rue d'YPRES. This was always satisfactory & was only used during the night.

A motor cyclist despatch riding post was established daily to HAZEBROUCK one post each way.

Feb 5th YPRES

Lt Skipwith joined at YPRES leaving the HAZEBROUCK office in charge of S.M. Norton. Communication satisfactory.

Sheet 5

WAR DIARY of 3rd Signal Squadron
or
INTELLIGENCE SUMMARY

Army Form C. 2118.

(Erase heading not required.)

Hour, Date, Place	Summary of Events and Information	Remarks and references to Appendices
Feb 6th YPRES	Lts Brudyll & Shipwith overhauled the lines to 7th Bde & on to 2nd Life Guards during the evening of 6th Feb. Nothing unusual during 6th Feb.	
Feb 7th YPRES	Signal Squadron interpreter (M. ESCUDIER) visited French Reserve exchange at HOOGE & reported everything satisfactory as regards French & British intercommunication; this liaison was in future carried out daily. Lt Shipwith continued lines from French Reserve (Cavan House) to 2nd Life Guards with D. cable thus giving 7th B de two lines to 2nd Life guards with the French Reserve Office "Veed" in our rear. The average number of messages dealt with daily mean for this week was	

AT YPRES | AT HAZEBROUCK
Incoming Outgoing | Incoming Outgoing
32 | 41 | 112 | 122

WAR DIARY of 3rd Signal Squadron
or
INTELLIGENCE SUMMARY

Army Form C. 2118.

Sheet 6

| Hour, Date, Place | Summary of Events and Information | Remarks and references to Appendices |

Feb 8th YPRES

Communication with F.C.O was broken during morning this was found to be due to a working party on the railway. Capt Fewtlough & Major Cavendish visited Gen Lefevre (18th French Div) at POTIJZE who was satisfied with intercommunication with French & British.

The 6th Brigade relieved the 4th Bde during the evening & the Brigade commander established his headquarters at the dug out where the 2nd Life Guards had been there doing away with the office North of ZILLEBEKE. The lines at the old 4th Bde H.Q. were "trunked" & this communication on two lines was established to the new 6th Bde H.Q.

The French Reserve Office (Canon House) was still "Kept in" to the lines.

Feb 9th YPRES

Communication to 6th Bde was not quite satisfactory during day but was improved on sending fresh materials to 6th Bde

SIGSKY

WAR DIARY of 3rd Signal Squadron

INTELLIGENCE SUMMARY

Army Form C. 2118.

Instructions regarding War Diaries and Intelligence Summaries are contained in F.S. Regs, Part II. and the Staff Manual respectively. Title pages will be prepared in manuscript.

(Erase heading not required.)

Hour, Date, Place	Summary of Events and Information	Remarks and references to Appendices
Feb 9th (continued)	As soon as dark. After this communication to 6th Bde was satisfactory but a great deal of repairing had to be done each night, this was carried out by L/s Bradyll & Shiputt with Pts Hurd & Stofer who all did good work. The Troop Officer 6th Bde laid a separate line this night to the French Reserve thus removing this office from YC/PF lines.	
Feb 10th YPRES	A good deal of shelling during the day & the line to PF was cut at 4pm but repaired by 5.30pm. During night the signal office was shelled & the top storey was vacated by the motor cyclists.	
Feb 11th YPRES	Nothing of interest. All communication satisfactory.	
Feb 12th YPRES	Nothing of interest. A great deal of induction on lines to PF & ECO; messages belonging to 28th Division were quite easily read on our instruments.	

Sheet 8

WAR DIARY of 3rd Signal Squadron
or
INTELLIGENCE SUMMARY

Army Form C. 2118.

(Erase heading not required.)

Hour, Date, Place	Summary of Events and Information	Remarks and references to Appendices
Feb 13th YPRES	Advanced party of 2nd Signal Squadron arrived at 6.30 am. Weather foggy so lines were handed over in daylight. At 5 pm O.C 2nd Signal Squadron arrived & took over. All lines & instruments in good order. 3rd Signal Squadron returned to old billets in HAZEBROUCK.	
Feb 14th HAZEBROUCK	The previous system of communication was re-established i.e Horse line to Cav Corps & three daily posts to Brigade & divisional troops. Captain Faulkner admitted to hospital. Leave to England for Officers men	
Feb 16th – Feb 28th HAZEBROUCK	The unit continued to occupy the same billets & the same system of communication was employed. Instruments damaged during the work in the	

March 1915
SDy
Fld

121/5204

War Diary

of the

3RD Signal Squadron
R.E.

for the

month of

3rd Cavalry Division.

March 1915.

Vol. IV

March 1915 Sheet 1.

WAR DIARY of 3rd Signal Squadron
or
INTELLIGENCE SUMMARY

Army Form C. 2118.

(Erase heading not required.)

Hour, Date, Place	Summary of Events and Information	Remarks and references to Appendices
March 1st HAZEBROUCK	Officers billets changed to 23 Rue de Clocher.	
March 2nd – 7th	Squadron remained in Billets at HAZEBROUCK. All communication to Brigades by motor cyclist. Instruction in unarmed work was given daily to certain drivers. On 7th F.G.C.M. on Dr Barnes was promulgated sentence five years penal servitude.	
March 8th & 9th	Nothing to record.	
March 10th	Squadron paraded in marching order & went for route march	
March 11th	No 3 & 2 reliefs paraded at 6.0am & proceeded to Divnl rendezvous at MOTTE AU BOIS establishing signal office at canal Bridge at 7.30am. Communication to all troops by motor cycle D.R. No 1 relief remaining in HAZEBROUCK	

Sheet 2

WAR DIARY of 3rd Signal Squadron Army Form C. 2118.
or
INTELLIGENCE SUMMARY
(Erase heading not required.)

Hour, Date, Place	Summary of Events and Information	Remarks and references to Appendices
	To keep communication with "Q" staff.	
	At 5pm Division went into Billets & mounted men of Squadron	
	returned to HAZEBROUCK.	
	Divisional HQ were established in Rue des CAPUCINES MERVILLE.	
	Cav Corps Signals gave a cable line from LAMOTTE to 1st Army	
	Report center (A.C.P) in MERVILLE & two operators were	
	found for the line in ACP office.	
	7th Bde were billeted at LES LAURIERS & a line was tapped on	
	to the 2CD/ACP line & the Signal troop officer was lent a	
	a vibrator & one operator.	
	Thus communication was as follows	
	To 2CD vibrator from ACP office	
	To PG ditto	
	To PF by a DR Head shakes 6th Bde was in MERVILLE.	

Sheet 3

WAR DIARY of 5rd Signal Squadron
or
INTELLIGENCE SUMMARY

Army Form C. 2118.

(Erase heading not required.)

Hour, Date, Place	Summary of Events and Information	Remarks and references to Appendices
March 11th MERVILLE	To PH by vibrator to 2CO & transmitted to VC in HAZEBROUCK and thence by DR to 8th Bde H.Q at farm ½ mile SW of G in Gde SEC BOIS	
	To RHA by vibrator to 2CO & thence by DR to Divn R.H.A HQ a distance of ½ mile. For this purpose two motor cyclists were put at disposal of 2CO	
	To Field Squadron via 2CO to VC in HAZEBROUCK & then by DR to their original billet.	
	Rations were brought from HAZEBROUCK in Sunbeam.	
March 12th	All remaining motor cyclists at HAZEBROUCK were brought to MERVILLE the office at VC being worked by one operator & mounted men. Rations were sent	

WAR DIARY of 3rd Signal Squadron Army Form C. 2118.

or

INTELLIGENCE SUMMARY

(Erase heading not required.)

Hour, Date, Place	Summary of Events and Information	Remarks and references to Appendices
March 12th MERVILLE	Up by lorry. Car copies lines via MERVILLE – ESTAIRE was reconnoitred in case of further advance. Only one officer remained night at MERVILLE others returned to HAZEBROUCK.	
March 13th MERVILLE	Same system of communication. Field Squadron moved to LE SART. Communication to them by D.R. At 4.15pm General Staff returned to HAZEBROUCK & VCR was closed; troops did not return to after dark & communication until their return to their old billets was via 2CO in case of RHA, & via 2CO +ACP in case of 6th Bde +Fd Squadron. 47th Bde	
March 14th HAZEBROUCK	Squadron remained in billets ready to move at 3 hours notice	
15th	Urgent messages sent to all units at 3.45am to be ready to move at two hours notice, General Staff office and A.A.QMG office connected by C2 telephone metallic circuit.	

Sheet 5

WAR DIARY of 3rd Signal Squadron

INTELLIGENCE SUMMARY

Army Form C. 2118.

(Erase heading not required.)

Instructions regarding War Diaries and Intelligence Summaries are contained in F. S. Regs, Part II. and the Staff Manual respectively. Title pages will be prepared in manuscript.

Hour, Date, Place	Summary of Events and Information	Remarks and references to Appendices
March 16th HAZEBROUCK	Orders received to be ready to move at four hours notice.	
March 17th "	Headquarters 8th Bde. at Chateau just E of EBBLINGHEM were connected to VC office using permanent line along railway. Connection being made to railway at BAR office. Morse Single current sets used on this line. Operators being lent to PH. It was found impossible to work VC intermediate with PH & 2CO, but signals with VC in lieu to both were excellent.	
March 18th "	Metallic telephone circuit HQ S/AAG was connected to R 2CO telephone exchange.	
March 19th "	Single current at PH was transferred to 4th Bde at RENESCURE still using the permanent railway air line.	

Sheet 6

WAR DIARY of 3rd Sig Squadron
or
INTELLIGENCE SUMMARY

Army Form C. 2118.

Hour, Date, Place	Summary of Events and Information	Remarks and references to Appendices
March 20th HAZEBROUCK	D¹ cable was laid between PH & PF using the Sniger which had been fitted up to carry ½ mile drums. This was most satisfactory & it was found that cable could easily be laid at 12 miles per hour without crossings. Subsequently OC 4th Div Sigs Troop Ycd in a line to 1st Life Guards at ERBLINGHEM. D3 F(ull) S(et) phones on this circuit.	
March 21st – 22nd	Nothing to record.	
March 23rd	A D¹ cable line to PF at STEENBECQUE was commenced using the Sniger as a cable cart. The line was laid to railway & then on along the hedges. Line had to be "poled" for distance of ½ mile.	
March 24th	Line continued to PF & worked with vibrator. Circuit diagram on this date attached.	Appendix A.

WAR DIARY
or
INTELLIGENCE SUMMARY

Army Form C. 2118.

Hour, Date, Place	Summary of Events and Information	Remarks and references to Appendices
March 25th - 31st	Nothing to record. Runs billets were changed in one instance as house had become unsanitary. Visual signalling instruction was carried out on five days. The following messages were dealt with during month. Average for seven days	

```
                Incoming  Outgoing  Urgent  Total
March  1st - 6th    88      144      14     232
       7 - 12th     84      162      19     246
      13 - 19th     93      159      18     252
      20 - 31st     78      163      11     241
```

J. M. Pantlong
Capt. RA.

Appendix A.

Circuit Diagram

24-3-15   V.C

RENESCURE STA   EBBLINGHEM A L G

PG — PH

RZCO exchange

V

ZCO LA MOTTE

G/S 3rd Cav Div
A.A QMG 3rd Cav Div

PF
STEENBECQUE

VC Signal Office
RZCO exchange   } HAZEBROUCK
G/S office
AAQMG office

S. N.F.

64

April & May - 1915

121/5496

3rd Cavalry Division

3rd Signal Squadron R.E.

Vol V   1.4 — 31.5.15.

Army Form A 2007.

CENTRAL REGISTRY.

Central Registry No. and Date.

Attached Files.

MAY & APRIL 1915

SUBJECT, AND OFFICE OF ORIGIN.

WAR DIARY
3RD SIGNAL SQDN' R.E.

Referred to	Date	Referred to	Date	Referred to	Date
				P.A.	Date

Schedule of Correspondence

Sheet I

April 1915

WAR DIARY
or
INTELLIGENCE SUMMARY of 3rd Signal Squadron

(Erase heading not required.)

Army Form C. 2118.

Instructions regarding War Diaries and Intelligence Summaries are contained in F. S. Regs., Part II. and the Staff Manual respectively. Title pages will be prepared in manuscript.

Hour, Date, Place	Summary of Events and Information	Remarks and references to Appendices
HAZEBROUCK April 1st	Visual Signalling practice	
2nd	Established helio cmn with 2CO from Pt 66 S.E. of HAZEBROUCK but failed to get PB on MONT des CATS owing to mist.	
3rd – 6th	Nothing special to record. Helio practice daily with 2CO from Pt 66. Weather damp & line to 2CO showed a good deal of earth- Ck about 100 poles for air lines from LAMOTTE.	
7th	Commenced to lay D. line from RENESCURE to 8th Bde HQ at BLARINGHEM.	
8th	Completed line PG/PH poled all the way	
9th	Tried to get helio cmn with RHA brigade at MT KEMMEL but Sun not strong enough.	
10th	Line's from EBBLINGHEM CHATEAU – RÉNESCURE picked up.	
11th–12th	Visual signalling practice	
13th	Laid a D. line for 8th Cavalry Bde at BLARINGHEM to Royal Horse Guards at LYNDE.	

Army Form C. 2118.

April Sheet 2

WAR DIARY
or
INTELLIGENCE SUMMARY of 3rd Signal Squadron

(Erase heading not required.)

Instructions regarding War Diaries and Intelligence Summaries are contained in F. S. Regs., Part II. and the Staff Manual respectively. Title pages will be prepared in manuscript.

Hour, Date, Place		Summary of Events and Information	Remarks and references to Appendices
HAZEBROUCK	April 15th	Squadron inspected in marching order by by O.C. who expressed himself satisfied.	
	16th–18th	Helio comm with 4th Bde R.H.A was established on these three days from fort blo to KEMMEL but required a Klinoscope for reading as the sun was never strong.	
	19th–20th	Nothing to record.	
	21st	LT. W V HOLT 12th Reserve Regt of Cavalry joined the unit.	
	22nd	Cable laying practice from limbered wagons; not successful, as the arms supporting the spindle were not strong enough & the drum constantly slipped out.	
	23rd	Division rendezvoused (ÉBREARDE) at 1.45pm and marched towards Ypres owing to sudden gas attack on the French lines N.W of YPRES. Reached ABEELE at 3pm and opened signal office. At 7.15pm Brigades ordered to billets as follows 6th Bde LETTRE 8th Bde ABEELE STA 7th Bde GODEWAERSVELDE Field Squadron ditto	

WAR DIARY or INTELLIGENCE SUMMARY of 3rd Signal Squadron

Army Form C. 2118.

April — Sheet 3

Hour, Date, Place	Summary of Events and Information	Remarks and references to Appendices
ABEELE — April 23rd (Cont)	Communication to Cav Corps (POPERINGHE) via R.T.O Telegraph office in ABEELE STATION. 10 mile by Div. The office at HAZEBROUCK was kept open for use of Q. Staff and Cav Corps transmitted messages via LA MOTTE	
April 24th	Ordered to move at 9.15 am to FM at cross roads ½ mile S of V of VLAMERINGHE. Established office there at 11.15 am. At 1.30 pm Cav Corps laid a line from WESTOUTRE and at 5.45 pm line was through. At 6.15 pm moved to WESTOUTRE and established Signal Office	
WESTOUTRE	At 7.15 pm in LAUNDRY of CONVENT. Communication for night as follows: 8th Brigade at BOESCHEPPE 7th Brigade at WESTOUTRE (by DR) Cavalry Corps at WESTOUTRE	8th Cav Brigade in farm ½ mile N of WESTOUTRE S Sqd V of VLAMERINGHE Field Squadron by visual through Cav Corps.
April 25th	Closed office at WESTOUTRE at 12 noon and opened at same hour at cross roads ½ mile due N of POPERINGHE. At 5.15 pm ordered to billet for night moved at once out to WINNEZEELE.	

WAR DIARY or INTELLIGENCE SUMMARY of 3rd Signal Squadron

Army Form C. 2118.

April

Hour, Date, Place	Summary of Events and Information	Remarks and references to Appendices
WINNEZEELE April 25th	Communication for night as follows: 6th Brigade at HOUTKERQUE 7th Brigade at crossroads A N of DROGLANDT } by DR. 8th Brigade at OUDEZEELE 3rd F Squadron at ditto S.A.A. Section at ditto To Cavalry Corps (CHAT. LOVIE) ON VISUALER by wire laid from Squadron to permanent line. 2ND Office at STEENVOORDE and teed on to permanent line.	
April 26th	At 11.30 am moved from WINNEZEELE and opened Signal office at Inn ½ St. 55 Routes W of POPERINGHE. At 2pm Cavalry Corps laid line to us from LOVIE CHATEAU worked thro' single circuit. At 8.15pm ordered to VLAMERTINGHE and opened office in Rue de BAILLEUL at 9.15pm Issuing office at Inn ½ St 55 8pm. Brigades were in huts just SOUTH of village and communication to Cav Corps was arranged through VBR who had an office in VLAMERTINGHE.	

WAR DIARY
or
INTELLIGENCE SUMMARY of 3rd Signal Squadron

Army Form C. 2118.

Week 5

(Erase heading not required.)

Instructions regarding War Diaries and Intelligence Summaries are contained in F. S. Regs., Part II. and the Staff Manual respectively. Title pages will be prepared in manuscript.

Hour, Date, Place	Summary of Events and Information	Remarks and references to Appendices
VLAMERINGHE April 27th	Division remained in vicinity of VLAMERINGHE and communication was as before. A certain amount of shelling and VBR evacuated to their office but returned later. R.I.A still at KEMMEL came by despatch rider down via 2RC & BAR.	
April 28th	Wires along railway shelled down — Cable wagon from cav reinfts laid a loop round village & so avoided using permanent line near station when shelling was always bad. 12 noon closed at VLAMERINGHE and moved back to our former office at Inn Pt 55 & Brigades moved back to their houses in that area. 6 k 7.30pm Divisional Headquarters moved for night to STEENVOORDE. Lt Skipwith remaining at office at Pt 55. Communication with CasCofps via YND office in STEENVOORDE also to Brigades from YND to 2RC & thus to Pt 55 — most satisfactory owing to transmission. LT BRADYLL 10th Cavalry I.A transferred to Base.	

Army Form C. 2118.

WAR DIARY
or
INTELLIGENCE SUMMARY of 3rd Signal Squadron

April

$\frac{5}{1}$ SS / 6

(Erase heading not required.)

Instructions regarding War Diaries and Intelligence Summaries are contained in F. S. Regs., Part II. and the Staff Manual respectively. Title pages will be prepared in manuscript.

Hour, Date, Place	Summary of Events and Information	Remarks and references to Appendices
April 29th	Closed office at STEENVOORDE 8.30 a.m. and opened at same hour at 1st SS – Same arrangements as before – Brigades all close. Returned to STEENVOORDE at 6.30 p.m. & got a direct line to 2RC (LOUIE CHAN). Left Lt HOLT at 1st SS to deliver by despatch rider to Brigades. Satisfactory time to Brigades was that VCR/2RC is a direct line. Transmitted to VAR at HOUT KERQUE for 2RC on vibrator.	
April 30th	Returned to 1st SS at 8.30 a.m. & remained there until 6.0 p.m. when H.Q. moved back to STEENVOORDE. Tried to work intermediate between VAR and 2RC but found it impossible so had to transmit to VAR on vibrator.	

P. Hawthorn
Capt RA
Cmdg 3rd Signal Squadron

WAR DIARY
or
INTELLIGENCE SUMMARY of 3rd Signal Squadron

Army Form C. 2118.

May

Sheet I

Hour, Date, Place	Summary of Events and Information	Remarks and references to Appendices
STEENVOORDE May 1st	Closed office at STEENVOORDE 8.30am and opened at same time at H/1st SS. Communication by morse to Cav Corps at LOVIE CHau & to Brigades by motor cyclists. At 6.30pm HQ returned to STEENVOORDE and office at H/1st SS was left open for communication to Brigades. Came in intermediate on morse between 2RC and VAR.	
May 2nd	Reopened at H/1st SS at 8.30am and returned to STEENVOORDE at 4/5pm. Same communication as on previous days.	
May 3rd	Remained at STEENVOORDE till 4pm at which hour orders were issued for HQ to move to HOUTKERQUE and arrangements were made for office at H/1st SS to close & move thus — however as soon as we started office at H/1st SS got through to Cav Corps on VLAMERTINGHE road. At 8.30pm Brigades arrived line HQ2 along railway with vibrators. At 10pm w/o dismounted and wire formed w/o dismounted East of VLAMERTINGHE.	

Army Form C. 2118.

WAR DIARY
or
INTELLIGENCE SUMMARY of 3rd Signal Squadron

S/Sdn 2.   May

(Erase heading not required.)

Instructions regarding War Diaries and Intelligence Summaries are contained in F.S. Regs, Part II. and the Staff Manual respectively. Title pages will be prepared in manuscript.

Hour, Date, Place	Summary of Events and Information	Remarks and references to Appendices
VLAMERINGHE May 3rd am	GOC spent night at 28th Division HQ (Chau VLAMERINGHE). Communication from there to Brigades by DR & to CavCorps established by wire back to LOVIE CHAU	
May 4th	Moved at 8.15am to HOUTKERQUE and took over Signal Office from CavCorps who had a line to LOVIE Chau Office at Pt 55 was closed & new brought to HOUTKERQUE. Communication to Brigades by dr Cavalry Corps (lent a double current set and so could work by dr Cavalry Corps) transmitting station at LOVIE being closed as direct to ZCO (LAMOTTE) Corps HQ returned to LAMOTTE.	
HOUTKERQUE May 5th	Remained at HOUTKERQUE communication as before. OC working party from Brigades proceeded mounted to YPRES for work on ramparts and a Divisional Report centre was established at 9pm at Pavn in Hill Pll 2.0am on 6th Communication to brigades by mounted despatch riders and motor cyclist.	
May 6th	dns from WINNEZEELE – STEENVOORDE was picked up by Singer. Pack wireless station arrived from CavCorps and communication with ZCO established at 7.45pm.	

1247 W 3299 200,000 (E) 8/14 J.B.C.&A. Forms/C.2118,11.

Army Form C. 2118.

WAR DIARY
or
INTELLIGENCE SUMMARY of 3rd Signal Squadron

(Erase heading not required.)

May

Hour, Date, Place	Summary of Events and Information	Remarks and references to Appendices
May 7th	Division returned to HAZEBROUCK area - duties to Brigades were found - work and communication as before.	
HAZEBROUCK May 8th	Lt Skipwith with party proceeded in Sunbeam to HOUTKERQUE and picked up Cavalry Corps line HOUTKERQUE - LOVIE CHAU	
May 9th	Division ordered to move by motorbus to VLAMERTINGHE. Left office open at HAZEBROUCK and opened report centre at 11.15am at level crossing on POPERINGHE - VLAMERTINGHE road between 4th & 8th kilostone. Test on to P74 (good line) & got come with ECO who transmitted to 2CO and VC (HAZEBROUCK). Had got 2CO on morse on at 6.30pm HQ clothed in farm. 7/4 Brigades were in huts LPR2 (a railway line) and ECO on P74 - Brigades were in huts just to the North and came to them by motorcyclist.	
YPRES May 15th	HQ remained in farm Hut. line lays on LTR2 had to be repaired - Satisfactory working to 2CO, took work for VAR.	

Army Form C. 2118.

WAR DIARY
or
INTELLIGENCE SUMMARY of 3rd Signal Squadron

(Erase heading not required.)

May   Sheet 4

Hour, Date, Place	Summary of Events and Information	Remarks and references to Appendices
YPRES May 11th	Remained at Farm Hud. Communication as on 10th	
May 12th	Orders that Division would take over trenches of 80th Bde. so 1st Skipwith laid line to Chateau on YPRES–MENIN road. This line ran through Vesting Station (K.G.H.W) close to LILLE Gate and so on to 80th Bde. HQ: line was doubled on left sides of L.G.H.W & was very useful on a subsequent occasion. Communication on vibrator to 27th Div (South of VLAMERTINGHE) was established on H92, also to 1st field Coy Bde by telephone at LILLE GATE. Instead of taking over lines of 80th Bde. division took over trenches between YPRES–ZONNEBEKE road and ROULERS railway left HQ of all Brigades at POTIJZE and communication was arranged through VAR/PD/PO also having HQ at POTIJZE).	
May 13th	1st Skipwith at 7.0am continued line from 80th Bde. to POTIJZE and under very heavy shelling got it through, very creditable performance. Owing to the situation G.O.C. moved to POTIJZE and three	

WAR DIARY or INTELLIGENCE SUMMARY of 3rd Signal Squadron

Army Form C. 2118.

May Sheet 5

Hour, Date, Place	Summary of Events and Information	Remarks and references to Appendices
May 13th	Motor cyclists were sent there in case the line PB/VAR was broken. It was found impossible to maintain the line to Farm Hud via 80th Bde owing to the shortage of linesmen and communication was restricted to the PB/VAR line which was quite satisfactory. During the heaviest part of the shelling Corporal HELLMUTH made three journeys in the Sunbeam from POTIJZE to Km West of YPRES and back back 17 wounded under shell fire.	
May 14th	Advanced report centre remained at POTIJZE. Communication with artillery very complete but not enough operators, especially as we had officers at HAZEBROUCK and Farm Hud. With help of 2nd Signal Troop managed to carry on, but too much work for a Signal Squadron establishment. About 3 pm a German advance was reported and within three minutes managed to get new forward batteries to open fire. Most fortunate that all artillery lines were intact as had they been broken there was only one lineman available to repair them. Division relieved at 9pm and HQ returned to Farm just West of YPRES.	

Army Form C. 2118.

WAR DIARY
or
INTELLIGENCE SUMMARY of 3rd Signal Squadron

Instructions regarding War Diaries and Intelligence Summaries are contained in F. S. Regs., Part II. and the Staff Manual respectively. Title pages Sheet 6 will be prepared in manuscript.

(Erase leading not required.)

Hour, Date, Place	Summary of Events and Information	Remarks and references to Appendices
May 15th	Moved to RENINGHELST at 12 noon. 5th Division in same village. Took on work for ECO until communication was established direct to ECO on 2W1 to POPERINGHE. Worked more to ECO but could not get 2CO direct so ECO transmitted. Brigades were bivouaced round VLAMERTINGHE and at 8pm got PF with vibrator on 2W2 and 7YH. Lt HOLT transferred to 6th Signal Troop in place of Captain Atkinson Royal Dragoons killed in action.	
RENINGHELST May 16th	Remained at RENINGHELST. Cavalry Corps Advanced report centre moved to WITTENHOEK and worked to us on 2W1 (ECO being cut out). PG came on the 7YH in place of PF and took work for three brigades at VLAMERTINGHE.	
RENINGHELST May 17th	Communication as on 16th.	
" May 18th	Cavalry Corps moved to LOVIE CHAM and we continued to work more on 2N1 in addition had a C2 telephone superimposed on 2N1 and 2N2. Following units were attached to division and communication was by relay: 28th Divisional Cyclists G11d 1S1stBde Hsd 4thBn E.Yorks LILLE GATE YPRES 2/8th Divisional Cyclists G12a 1Sqdn Surrey Yeomanry	

1247 W 3299 200,000 (E) 8/14 J.B.C.&A. Forms/C. 2118 F.C.

Army Form C. 2118.

WAR DIARY
or
INTELLIGENCE SUMMARY. of 3rd Signal Squadron

(Erase heading not required.)

Instructions regarding War Diaries and Intelligence Summaries are contained in F. S. Regs., Part II and the Staff Manual respectively. Title pages will be prepared in manuscript.

Sheet 7

Place	Date May	Hour	Summary of Events and Information	Remarks and references to Appendices
RENINGHELST	19th		Remained at RENINGHELST. Communication as on 18th.	
" "	20th		Nothing to record. Cavalry Corps laid a cable from their day report centre in H15 a/c to our signal office - Brigades still at VLAMERTINGHE and PG received work for all three.	
" "	21st		Brigades left VLAMERTINGHE at 9pm by motor bus for their billets in HAZEBROUCK area - 1st Skt with and two sqadrons remained for night at 21st/R2nd at RENINGHELST remainder of Squadron returned to HAZEBROUCK	
HAZEBROUCK	22nd		Nothing to record.	
" "	23rd		Divisional Headquarters moved to RENESCURE - got a line along railway from GCP (HAZEBROUCK) and to worked to 2CD - Used old PG/PH lines to work Vibrator to PH.	
RENESCURE	24th		All Squadron moved to RENESCURE. Signal office established next the post office where there was a civilian French Exchange (telephone) which we took	

Army Form C. 2118.

WAR DIARY
or
INTELLIGENCE SUMMARY of 3rd Signal Squadron Sheet 6

(Erase heading not required.)

Instructions regarding War Diaries and Intelligence Summaries are contained in F. S. Regs., Part II. and the Staff Manual respectively. Title pages will be prepared in manuscript.

Place	Date	Hour	Summary of Events and Information	Remarks and references to Appendices
	May			
RENESCURE	24th		Possession of and laid metallic circuits to G.S and A.G.s offices. Could get 2CO via HAZEBROUCK civil exchange and also PC at WARDRECQUES.	
"	25th		Laid line from TH at BLARINGHEM to PF at MORBECQUE 10 PH transmitted to PF.	
"	26th		Rested up line HAZEBROUCK – STEENBECQUE.	
"	27th 28th		Nothing to record. Lines of 2nd Cavalry Division from BIENFAISSANCE to forward trenches reconnoitred.	
"	29th		Division moved by motorbus to YPRES to take over trenches from 2nd Cavalry Division Signal Squadron/ New office left at RENESCURE/ Took over cavalry Corps Signal office in Farm H 15 a/c. Cavalry Corps had three operators. Lines taken over were as follows – twin lines (one cable and one airline) to 8th Bde HQ at BIENFAISSANCE line to ZRC (LOVIE CHAN) 930 on to ECO and 2CO line to 27# Bn CRA	

Army Form C. 2118.

WAR DIARY
or
INTELLIGENCE SUMMARY of 3rd Signal Squadron

Instructions regarding War Diaries and Intelligence Summaries are contained in F.S. Regs., Part II. and the Staff Manual respectively. Title pages will be prepared in manuscript.

(Erase heading not required.)

Month: May

Place	Date	Hour	Summary of Events and Information	Remarks and references to Appendices
	May			
VLAMERTINGHE	29th		One line to 5th Div at RENINGHELST. In addition there were lines to 27 & 28th Divisions worked by their own operators.	
—	30th		Made arrangements to hand over signal office to 3rd Division and sent two linemen to "GOLDFISH CHAU" in H'd to take over from 2nd Cavalry Division.	
YPRES	31st		At 8.15am handed over to 3rd Division office to CHAU in H'd. Had the following lines. Double line through LGHW to TH in BIENFAISSANCE, this was the line laid previously by the squadron. Morse line to ECO and 2CO. Metallic telephone circuit to ERC exchange. Vibrator line to HQBW at VLAMERTINGHE. Vibrator line to 3rd Division. At 5pm Cavalry Corps had a bulk and airlines to TH through LGHW and this was used for C2 telephone circuit. Note — A fuse line exchange should be issued to signal squadrons.	

E.H. Fawthorp
Capt R.A.
3rd Signal Squadron

3rd Cavalry Division June 1915

Army Form A 2007.

CENTRAL REGISTRY.

Central Registry No. and Date.

Attached Files. 121/6390

JUNE 1915

SUBJECT, AND OFFICE OF ORIGIN.

WAR DIARY
3RD SIGNAL SQD'N RE.

Referred to	Date	Referred to	Date	Referred to	Date
		Vol VI			
				P.A.	Date

Schedule of Correspondence

WAR DIARY or INTELLIGENCE SUMMARY

of 3rd Signal Squadron

Sheet I

Army Form C. 2118.

June

Place	Date	Hour	Summary of Events and Information	Remarks and references to Appendices
YPRES	June 1st		Headquarters in Chan on YPRES-POPERINGHE road - Communication to Brigades in ECOLE de BIENFAISANCE by vibrator and C.R. telephone on two lines passing through L.G.H.W. To F.C.O & R.C.O. by morse (F.C.O intermediate), also metallic circuit telephone via F.C.R. exchange on PK1 & PK2 - To 3rd Div and 4th BW by vibrator. All lines Sato factory	
	2nd	About 4.30pm	both lines to ECOLE were broken by shell fire but communication was maintained through 3rd Division and 9th Inf Bde Both lines were repaired by linemen in L.G.H.W. The airline being cut in several places between L.G.H.W & the ECOLE. LUCKNOW Cavalry Brigade attached to Division. Communication to them on vibrator on PYH to their Headquarters in VLAMERTINGHE.	
	3rd		Nothing to record. All communication Satisfactory - at 9pm by O.C moved to ECOLE & remained there till 8am on 4th. A small party went to ECOLE but were not employed as 8th Bde Signal Troop did all the communications.	

WAR DIARY
or
INTELLIGENCE SUMMARY.

Army Form C. 2118.

of 3rd Signal Squadron
June 1915
Sheet 2

Place	Date	Hour	Summary of Events and Information	Remarks and references to Appendices
YPRES	June 4th		Nothing to record.	
	5th		Communication as on previous days – 7th Cavalry Brigade relieved by infantry and do office (PG) in YPRES Ramparts closed at 9pm.	
	6th		Division relieved and returned to billets HQ at RENESCURE. Air line to ECOLE was dismantled and returned to Cav Corps Signals. Remaining lines handed over to 3rd Division but no wire received in exchange. Four men allowed leave to ENGLAND period 72 hours.	
RENESCURE	7th		Lines to Brigades found intact but required repairing in places – Civilian telephone exchange most useful.	
	8th		At 2.15am heavy thunderstorm succeed lightening lobbins fired but no damage to instruments.	

Army Form C. 2118.

WAR DIARY
or
INTELLIGENCE SUMMARY. of 3rd Signal Squadron

Sheet 3 June

(Erase heading not required.)

Instructions regarding War Diaries and Intelligence Summaries are contained in F. S. Regs., Part II. and the Staff Manual respectively. Title pages will be prepared in manuscript.

Place	Date	Hour	Summary of Events and Information	Remarks and references to Appendices
RENESCURE	June 9th, 10th		⎱ Nothing to record ⎰	
	11th		Wire from PH (BLARINGHEM) to PF (STEENBECQUE) laid. The previous route was pulled - could not work direct to PF instead of PH transmitting	
	12th		Nothing to record	
	13th		Sergt. Norton transferred to Cavalry Corps Signals.	
	14th - 21st		All communication satisfactory.	
	22nd		Inspection of interpreters (French) - Brigadier ESCUDIER 31st Dragoons paraded mounted. Sergt PRESTON and Pvt HURD mentioned in despatches -	
	23-24th		Nothing to record	
	25th		Electric lamp reading by day. Quite satisfactory at 500 yds in dull light.	

1577 Wt.W10791/1773 500,000 1/15 D.D.&L. A.D.S.S./Forms/C. 2118.

Army Form C. 2118

WAR DIARY
or
INTELLIGENCE SUMMARY of 3rd Signal Squadron

June
Sheet 4

(Erase heading not required.)

Instructions regarding War Diaries and Intelligence Summaries are contained in F. S. Regs., Part II. and the Staff Manual respectively. Title pages will be prepared in manuscript.

Place	Date	Hour	Summary of Events and Information	Remarks and references to Appendices
	June			
RENESCURE	28th		Class of 15 men from the Regiments of the Division arrived for instruction in Buzzer Reading, Lineman's work. Divided into two classes. "A" those who already knew alphabet & "B" the remainder.	
	29th		Instruction of class commenced and all seemed keen to learn — each class had five hours buzzer practice a day and one hour's lecture on electricity, magnetism on alternate days, instruction in cable laying and lineman's duties. N.C.O.s returned from Pigeon flying course	
	30th		Men fully occupied with class who seem very keen & results should be good. All communication, on satisfactory in spite of wet weather during preceding three days.	

R H Hawthorn
Capt
3rd S.S. Squadron

July - 1915

3rd Signal Squadron

WAR DIARY
or
INTELLIGENCE SUMMARY.

Army Form C. 2118

3 Squadron

July 1915

Place	Date	Hour	Summary of Events and Information	Remarks and references to Appendices
RENESCURE	11th — 11th		Luisenni Class had a secondary line to P.H. Tonight I had telegraph poles with and without climbing irons. Faults in line.	
	12th		Sent two signal stations to No. 4 in LONGUENESSE (S.A. Haytrurood) to signal with the Belgian battery which was giving an exhibition of firing for G.H.Q. extrication.	
	13		At FAIRTLOUGH commenced laying a D.3 line from WARDRECQUES towards Helfant. Sent another party also to the Forêt de CLAIRMARAIS to cut poles. Headquarters moves from Renescure. Yesterday's line had been started and work recommenced in the wrong direction.	
PIHEM	14th		other east of the village. As soon as possible another party commenced laying back towards the other. They met in BLEQUES about 5.30 p.m. It had rained hardly since 2 p.m. Our Corps Air line which was due to be finished at 11 a.m. was not completed before nightfall, as kept open at Renescure.	
	15th		Improved yesterday's line and joining a line to the staff at Grand Bois Cap Lofs in line through by 6 p.m. having at discretion to a circle to get to us. Closed office in Renescure. R.H.A. brought us in a line from Pihem Majority of Divisional details in HEURINGHEM so had to establish a Brigade office there (V.C.R.)	

Army Form C.

WAR DIARY
or
INTELLIGENCE SUMMARY. 3 Signal Squadron

July 1915.

(Erase heading not required.)

Instructions regarding War Diaries and Intelligence Summaries are contained in F. S. Regs., Part II. and the Staff Manual respectively. Title pages will be prepared in manuscript.

Place	Date	Hour	Summary of Events and Information	Remarks and references to Appendices
PIHEM	15th		Gen. Staff GRAND BOIS. ADMS	
			A & V Signals PIHEM ADVS	
			OC ASC GRAND BOIS APM HEURINGHEN	
			7th Tn Rde WARDRECQUES DADOS	
			6th Cav Rde STEENRECQUES CHAPLAIN	
			8th Cav Rde BLARINGHEM RHA BILQUES	
			3rd Field Squadron QUIESTEDE Supply Column MORBECQUES	
			Ammunition Park	
			Duty of collecting and delivering the mails put on to the Signal Squadron. Had to send no 12 and 4 into ST OMER	
	16th		Continued given line from Bilques to Heuringhen and put in a late pole.	
			Another party reeled up part of the gunner line and relaid it on the opposite side of the road, as there had been such heavy interference between the two.	

WAR DIARY

INTELLIGENCE SUMMARY. 3 Signal Squadron

July 1915

Date	Hour	Summary of Events and Information	Remarks and references to Appendices
17th		One party laid a line down canal from PG to PH, as soon as that was strung a second party commenced reeling up from Rousseure to Blaringhem on J3 line and one D1 line. Did not finish work till nearly 6.30 and not both till 7.30 and it had been raining heavily.	
18th		Both linesmen's electrodes sent to rejoin their units. Water was scarce and the only exercise horses got was going down to Wyzerne. Three times a day, which totalled up about 14 kilometres.	
21st		A strong party ordered to Fluerdinghe to dig trenches for L & NW telegraph and cable with them and arranged with VI Corps to take telegraph messages for them	
24		Lt FAIRCLOUGH designed and built a trailer for reeling up cable, so lower to be raised by the car. The winding gear operated by the tread wheel of a motorcycle, with the clutch and brake speeds to regulate the rate of revolution of the drum.	
		An adverse report made by the ADVS on the condition of our horses. In Captain .... received and a clerk kept in .... NCO struck off Signal duty till a change should be seen.	

Army Form C. 2118.

WAR DIARY
or
INTELLIGENCE SUMMARY.
(Erase heading not required.)

Instructions regarding War Diaries and Intelligence Summaries are contained in F. S. Regs., Part II. and the Staff Manual respectively. Title pages will be prepared in manuscript.

3 Signal Squadron   July 1915

Place	Date	Hour	Summary of Events and Information	Remarks and references to Appendices
	26th		Captain Faithfull discovered that over 900 francs had been stolen out of his dispatch case.	
	27th		Visual practice.	
	28th		Established visual communication with P6 from Pekin having one transmitting station on the ridge at IE BIBELOT.	
	29-30th		Visual practice, also telegraph operators as well.	

C. Shipwith M.C.
3 Signal Squadron.

3rd Cavalry Division

121/6787

3rd Signal Squadron R.E.

Vol VII

August 15

AUG. 1915

Army Form C. 2118.

WAR DIARY
or INTELLIGENCE SUMMARY.
(Erase heading not required.)

3 SIGNAL SQUADRON
AUGUST 1915

Place	Date	Hour	Summary of Events and Information	Remarks and references to Appendices
PIHEM	2.8.15		Visual reading practice for R.O. Operators	
	4.8.15		Commenced laying D₅ line from DENNEBROEUCQ to FAUQUEMBERGUES. Laid D1 metallic circuit from DENNEBROEUCQ to WANDONNE chateau	
	5.8.15		Reeled up D3 line from BILQUES to HEURINGHEM and then completed metallic circuit between D + F into two miles D5 and two miles D3.	
	6.8.15		Reeled up D3 line from WARDRECQUES to PIHEM. and found that our "trailer" was most useful, the latter is towed behind the car and consists of a light wooden framework mounted on motor cycle wheels. The operation of 1½ years winds the drum. Reeled up D1 circuit to General Staff and AA & QMG. Division moved into its new billeting area and units were located as under.	

General Staff .... Chateau WANDONNE
A.A.Q.M.G. .... ECOLE DENNEBROEUCQ
3 Signal Squadron ... ECOLE DENNEBROEUCQ

WAR DIARY or INTELLIGENCE SUMMARY

Army Form C. 2118.

AUGUST 1915. 3 Signal Squadron

(Erase heading not required.)

Place	Date	Hour	Summary of Events and Information	Remarks and references to Appendices
RENNEBROEUCQ	6.8.15		OC ASC APM CAMP COMMANDANT CHAPLAIN DADOS ADMS ADVS PG PF PH HD SANITARY SECTION B ECHELON CFA } FAUQUEMBERGUES VCR Office established in civil post office for receiving & delivering messages. Personnel 1 operator, linesman, cyclist. Chateau at FEBVIN-PALFART 3 FIELD SQUADRON — BOMY — WANDONNE — RADINGHEM SUPPLY COLUMN — ERNY ST JULIEN AMMUNITION PARK — ARQUES AMMUNITION COLUMN — ENQUIN LES MINES — COUPELLE VIEILLE	

Army Form C. 2118.

WAR DIARY
or
INTELLIGENCE SUMMARY.   3 Signal Squadron
(Erase heading not required.)

AUGUST 1915

Place	Date	Hour	Summary of Events and Information	Remarks and references to Appendices
DENNEBROEUCQ	7.8.15		Laid a metallic D3 circuit from FLECHIN P.O. to P.F.	
	9.8.15		3 Field Squadron moved to VINCLY	
			Reeled up D3 line on canal between HARDRECQUES & BLARINGHEM and D' line between BLARINGHEM & STEENBECQUE	
	12.8.15		Arrangements made with Signals YER to accept messages for the divisional troops who were digging entrenchments at ARMENTIERES. One motorcyclist left at 6 p.m. daily from S.O. opening the night and returning the following morning	
	13.8.15		Commenced laying an iron wire line to WANDONNE	
	14.8.15		Completed this line and took it into use in place of the D1	
	17 – 24		By lifting an iron wire metallic circuit from S.O to FAUQUEMBERGUES and took it into use at 1 p.m. on 24th	
	25.8.15		Laid a D3 line from PRO to 4 VCR to PG and connected it through on the D5 line to VC working a vibrator on it.	
	30.8.15		Reeled up the one drum of D5 and one drum D3 from VCR to VC Captain Fairtlough R.A. relinquished command of this squadron and joined 121st Battery R.F.A.	

C. J. Richmond Jr. ???

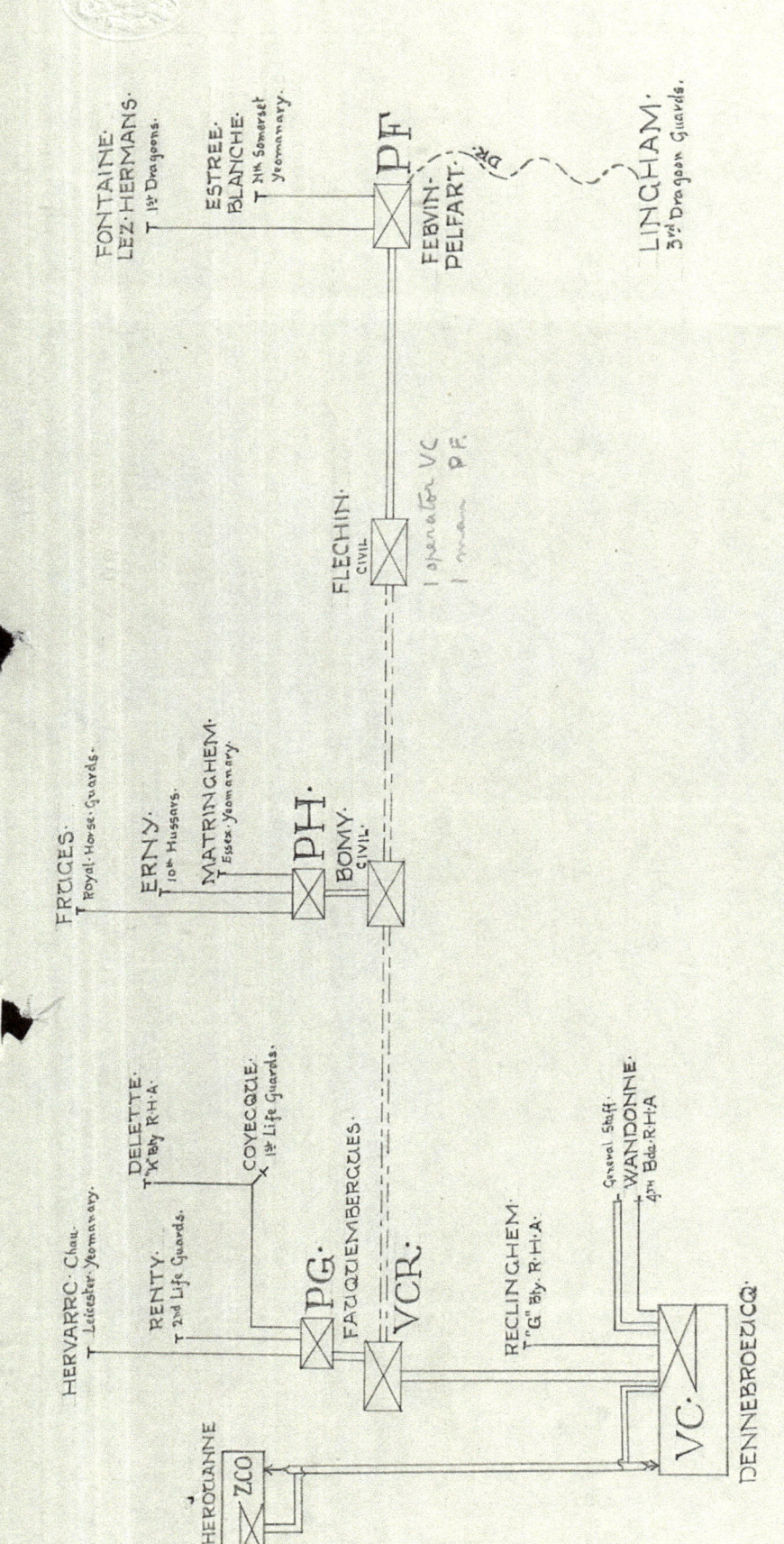

2/7341

SEPT-1915

3rd Cavalry Division

3rd Signal Squadron R.E.

Vol VIII

SEPT 1915

Army Form C. 2118.

WAR DIARY

SEPTEMBER 1915. INTELLIGENCE SUMMARY. 3 Signal Squadron R.E.

(Erase heading not required.)

Place	Date	Hour	Summary of Events and Information	Remarks and references to Appendices
JENNEBROEUCQ	1	7¹	Headquarters and batteries of 4ᵗʰ Bde R.H.A. moved as follows: Headquarters to HINGES "C" Battery HINGES "K" Battery HINGES "G" Battery LES BREBIS near MAZINGARBE AMMUNITION COLUMN LENGLET U 22 A Sheet	
	3	2ⁿᵈ	LT C SKIPWITH 17TH CAVALRY on returning from leave took over command of the squadron.	
	6	1ˢᵗ	Cavalry Corps and 3rd Cav. division practiced co-operation between aeroplanes, a representative from Bde Hqtrs attended. One machine dropped two messages; they fell about 400 & 500 yards from the mark but were seen to drop and no difficulty was experienced in picking up the messages. Height of machine was 1000 feet.	
	8	11¹	A Corps scheme of communications was held in conjunction with a scheme for the General Staff.	

Army Form C. 2118.

WAR DIARY
or
INTELLIGENCE SUMMARY.
(Erase heading not required.)

September 1915.   3 Signal Squadron

Place	Date	Hour	Summary of Events and Information	Remarks and references to Appendices
DENNEBRŒUCQ	8th		VCR was established at C in EREHEM Sheet 5A at 8 am and a D1 wire was laid at 7 am from DOHEM to VCR being completed at 8 AM. Communication with Cavalry Corps was established by telephone (overhead) at 8.30 AM. The idea was that a gap had been forced and no wheeled traffic was permissible, so all equipment had to be carried on the man or horse. Wire one was opened into Cav Corps Station at HELFAUT at 10.15 AM and with VSR at W in WISQUES at 10.30 AM. A pigeon station (6 birds) from AIRE was attached to VCR and a relief of 2 more birds was sent up later. A timed received messages from an aeroplane operating in advance of the Corps. One mounted DR was received and sent to 2RC at THEROUANNE. *Mistake* First battery pigeons Reeled up D1 wire laid out yesterday.	
	9th			

Army Form C. 2118.

WAR DIARY
or
INTELLIGENCE SUMMARY. 3 Signal Squadron

September 1915

(Erase heading not required.)

Place	Date	Hour	Summary of Events and Information	Remarks and references to Appendices
DENNEBROEUCQ	9th		Captain P. Brocklehurst, 1st Life Guards, took over 7th Signal Troop from Lt. Drake, 11th Hussars, who proceeded to join Cavalry Corps Signal as Pigeon Officer.	
	10th		Conference at Cav. Corps on the scheme of instruction. Various proposals made. Strong representations made that Signal Squadrons should have their establishment of visual signallers increased.	
	11th		Arrangements made for communication fr. 4th Rbde RHA, from Col and G Battery should be sent to ACP office at HINGES and collected from there.	
	13th		Marching order parade, followed by a route march.	
	17th		Wireless and aeroplane scheme into Carolphe and Slyndus. ZRE established tomorrow. VBR Rreginghem V.C.R. Blendecques. Got one message by wireless and that after noon when we had practically closed down. From out a wire to VBR for practice but had to reel it up almost directly. It was finished but not 25 miles by the time we got back and the horses fell to the violence.	

1577 Wt.W10791/1773 500,000 1/15 D.D.&L. A.D.S.S./Forms/C. 2118.

Army Form C. 2☐

WAR DIARY
or
INTELLIGENCE SUMMARY.
(Erase heading not required.)

Instructions regarding War Diaries and Intelligence Summaries are contained in F. S. Regs., Part II. and the Staff Manual respectively. Title pages will be prepared in manuscript.

September 3 Signal Squadron 1915

Place	Date	Hour	Summary of Events and Information	Remarks and references to Appendices
DENNEBROEUCQ	18th		Experimented with visibility of different coloured screens and flags with a view to indicating advanced cavalry from to his of their own Army.	
	20th		It was decided that each troop should carry a white screen 15ft by 4ft, this to signify that the troop was in action 300 yards in front. In the afternoon an aeroplane dropped messages all of which were received except as which dropped into a wood. Signor Marconi visited Cavalry Corps Signals and various wireless exhibitions and experiments were shown in his honour. This was followed by a signal conference to settle various questions of procedure in case of certain eventualities happening.	
	21st		3 Cav.Div. is placed direct under the orders of the First Army. No arrangements were made with the 4th troops as LABUISSIERE for the use of their lines back to A.C.P. At 11 am advanced party started under Lt FAIRCLOUGH. Ruled up line of D5 to Fauquembergue also D3 into town. Disconnected a line of D1 belonging to PA from Berry to Fruges. Ruled up line of D3 from Aseline Post Office to Estrain - Raffaut.	

1577 Wt.W10791/1773 500,000 1/15 D. D. & L. D. D. & L. A.D.S.S./Forms/C. 2118.

WAR DIARY or INTELLIGENCE SUMMARY

Army Form C. 2118

3 Sig Squad September 1915.

Place	Date	Hour	Summary of Events and Information	Remarks and references to Appendices
JENNEBROEUCQ	6th		Cav Bde moved down on night of 20th - 21st to bivouacs in the Bk Cav Bde.	
	7th		Two Bde was placed under orders of 2nd Army and moved off on 21st. B Echelons moved to WESTREHEM. 2CO delivering for us. 21st 22nd } BOIS DES DAMES.	
LABUSSIERE	22nd		Recd up D1 line from Bomy to Inges.	
	23rd		and General Staff moved. Opened office at 10 am close office office in by chateau LABUSSIERE. Telephonic communication with PF, PH, AC, GS, and DCO exchange. Communicated with Cav Corps via figure bf exchange in Lorinine, Landon, Depot to Therouanne. Visited AEP, ACO, DCO, YAR to ascertain what arrangements they had made for normal communication forward.	
	24th		Took over + Run & left R 29 birds from Merville. They average 40 minutes for flight from Vermelles. The quickest being 17 minutes. Message was taken to 100 and wired from there to ACP. Ready to move off by 5:30 am. Car went in and brought 16 birds from Merville. Received orders at 8:30 am to move up to VAUDRICOURT to	
	25th		HQ of Advanced Fourth Corps (DR C).	

WAR DIARY
or
INTELLIGENCE SUMMARY.

Army Form C. 2118

3 Signal Squadron

September 1915.

Place	Date	Hour	Summary of Events and Information	Remarks and references to Appendices
MAZINGARBE	25th	At 11.30 am orders to move forward left, two operators with D.R.C. advanced via Road and then on to Road 6. These had been specially prepared and marked out for the cavalry to advance up free of obstacles. Headquarters stopped just N. of railway embankment and 100 yards W. of the HALTE.	Advanced
		At 1.10 P.M.	they moved to the headquarters of Advanced 1st Div. (Y.O.R.) at MAZINGARBE. Squadron had got rather scattered in the advance partly all arrived with the exception of the RE Linesmen waggon. Cloudy & misty all the morning and rain fell late in the afternoon. Van Y.O.R. office for an evening. Arranged connected General Staff by telephone on to the D.A.C. exchange in cellars of MAZINGARBE Chateau.	
	26th	Standing to at 5.20 am. Transport & Echelon arrived up A1 and to the followed up with the horses and the latter moved parked under cover on G.	
		Noon 4.30 P.M. 6th Cav. Bde. ordered forward. Kept R.E. two operators and two linesmen. They went as far as Quatretstrasses. Hence forward to find line trenches and later to Loos where we got out of touch with them. Ran a line across to Quality Street. The R.H.Q. put themselves in communication with CRAY at 1500 Dan Mon. 30 PM. General decided to move up to LOOS with	

A.D.S.S./Forms/C. 2118.

WAR DIARY or INTELLIGENCE SUMMARY

Army Form C. 2118.

September 1915 Signed [Squadron?]

Place	Date	Hour	Summary of Events and Information	Remarks and references to Appendices

26th — Remainder of the division took up a small party of cyclists in to LOOS and formed 6th Role established in cellar of YDE with a line to YDE and DRC also a wire to LOOS station. Mr Finlays brigade in a D5 line from Quality Street (YOD) to LOOS front line at 1.30 am. It was not strong. Men sent to P.F. Mayer at Quality Street as a telegy station. Signal office in a cellar opposite to General Staff. A German exchange (10 line) left in position or taken together with magnets and two German bells. Two dead Germans in the cellar but had them shifted out in the morning. 8th Cav Bde arrived in the village just before dawn.

LOOS 27th — Started working back towards Quality Street to put second line through and to organize communications with the Corps. Relied up line from YORT to Quality Street with drew party. And office from YOR to grounds of Helen used by DAC. Took some men up to LOOS with me. Went down a German communication trench, full of dead, because a machine gun opened to be playing on the Cemetery Rt Horrte Guards made an attack and LOOS got shelled badly, so all brigades for 1½ hours. Gas shells were used and the men refused to advance to dun then smoke helmets.

Army Form C. 2118.

WAR DIARY
or
INTELLIGENCE SUMMARY.   3rd Signal Squadron
(Erase heading not required.)

September 1915

Instructions regarding War Diaries and Intelligence Summaries are contained in F.S. Regs., Part II. and the Staff Manual respectively. Title pages will be prepared in manuscript.

Place	Date	Hour	Summary of Events and Information	Remarks and references to Appendices
LOOS	27th		Apparent of lines hit several times. General staffs have brought down on top of them, no one hurt. General Briggs was in a cellar at the time. The 14th Sr. Rode had an office in Loos also and their line to the 47th Div was nearly always through so we kept an orderly there to take messages as ... Br. ESCUDIER accompanied Cpl Hellmuth with an ro two. They were greeted at the church by an H.E and Cpl Hellmuth was wounded in the foot having time bred and probably further damage to his foot. VAR brought in a line to the office ready for work to 2B when it should relieve us Regtl. two Leinmen and a M.C at Quarely stood ro that we might use it in case other broke down. We were able to use it on two occasions though V A exchange, when we could now get things to DRC direct.	
	28th		Fairly Quiet in the morning and sent Linemen out to get a third line through to the Corps but there was such a muddle of lines that they did not succeed in doing it, though they were out all the morning. About 3.45 there was another attack of the Guards and enemy took all their lines were broken by falling houses etc. Repair	

1577   Wt.W10791/1773   500,000   1/15   D.D.&L.   A.D.S.S./Forms/C. 2118.

WAR DIARY
INTELLIGENCE SUMMARY.

Army Form C. 2118

3 Signal Squadron

September 1915

(Erase heading not required.)

Place	Date	Hour	Summary of Events and Information	Remarks and references to Appendices
LOOS	28th		Officers had forward difficulty owing to the mass of debris covering them. There were only "div" lines to them and when 2B came up to relieve us about 11 pm all lines were working with the exception of the RHA line for whom I had no linesmen left to assist. The King Signals came up the main road to help carry away the telephones, wireless and a german exchange. Relief was completed at 2 A.M. The men walked back to MAZINGARBE.	
LABUISSIERE	29th		Closed our office in MAZINGARBE and marched to LABUISSIERE and took up our quarters in the small chateau.	
	30th		Worked to PF on an old line which we had new-taken up and allowed him to be his regiments onto an old P/L line fourth corps had run a line (R.A) running to P.H in chateau at GOSNAY. The ADMS 15th Div. was also on this line which I brought the DCo exchange. Diverted the old P/L line to new office and cheesed up old PF line. Ran an telephone lines for OS. in small chateau and He in big chateau. Cossacks amongst motor cycles were five in number.	

Army Form C. 2?

WAR DIARY
or
INTELLIGENCE SUMMARY. 3 Signal Squadron

September 1915

(Erase heading not required.)

Place	Date	Hour	Summary of Events and Information	Remarks and references to Appendices
	30th		Recommended No 29618 Motorcyclist Cpl Smith E.V. No 27309 Sapper Whyte W.T. No 25540 Driver Hardy J.C. for excellent work done during these operations and on previous occasions. Recommended No 3924 Acting Cpl Hellmuth F.A. ASC for gallant conduct on May 13th for conveying wounded from Potijze under shell fire	

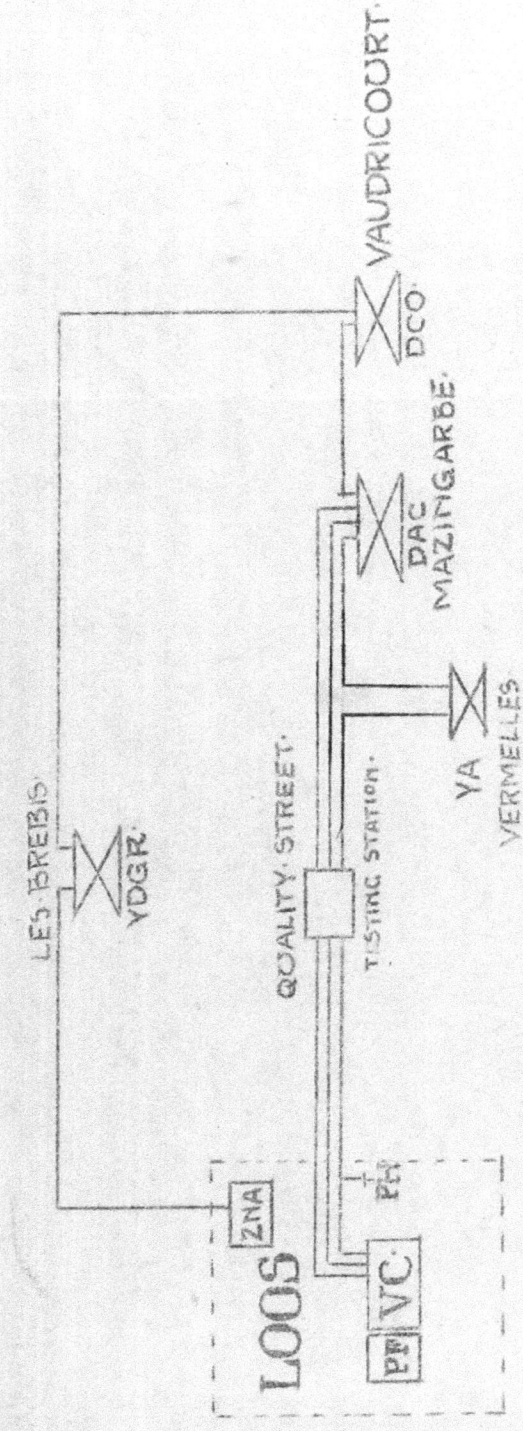

CIRCUIT DIAGRAM.
3RD SIGNAL SQUADRON. SEPT. 27. 1915.

121/7466

Oct 1915.

3rd Cavalry Division

3rd Signal Squadron R.E.

8 Dec 16

Vol IX

WAR DIARY or INTELLIGENCE SUMMARY

Army Form C. 2118

October 1915 — 3 Signal Squadron

Place	Date	Hour	Summary of Events and Information	Remarks and references to Appendices
LABUISSIERE	1st	8 am	Cav Bde moved from Gosnay to Labeuvriere between the two places as we merely joined up the two lines already in existence.	
	3rd		Report centre opened at HURIONVILLE woods reads at 10.20 am. Closed down own office at 11 am and ran up line to PF & local circuits. DC moving to their old quarters here and leaving VAUDRICOURT. Took over the 2RC line from VBR in ECQUEDECQUES at 3.30 PM. An old DS line lying along the road between Bruaire and us was brought completed the line into D3 and repaired and lined to rest. All headquarter units billeted in the village. 6th Cav Bde at FERFAY 8th Cav Bde at BURBURE Ammunition Park AUCHEL 3rd Field Squadron at BURBURE Supply Column LILLERS	
ECQUEDECQUES	4th		Ran a D3 cable line from Hurionville to Ferfay. Worked virator over this line to PF, PH. Telephonic communication with the Corps by means of a switch. Called up on morse and asked to speak on the telephone. Heard that a damaged motorbike had been brought back from loss by one of the motor ambulances. It was at the P.A.W. & works lot and we identified it as Sgt SHAW'S.	

Army Form C. 2118.

WAR DIARY
or
INTELLIGENCE SUMMARY.   3 Signal Squadron

(Erase heading not required.)

Instructions regarding War Diaries and Intelligence Summaries are contained in F.S. Regs., Part II and the Staff Manual respectively. Title pages will be prepared in manuscript.

October 1915

Place	Date	Hour	Summary of Events and Information	Remarks and references to Appendices
ECQUEDECQUES	8th		Cable line 6 ZRC replaced by an air line. Taken in to use in the afternoon but was not satisfactory so continued to work on the old line till morning.	
	9th		Lt Fenthorpe made an improvised bugger exchange out of cartridge cases with improvised holes for plugs. Sent it to the troops for use.	
	11th		Reeled up Corps line from our office in to KILLERS and kept the cable for further use. Suddenly heard quite by accident that headquarters were going to move their billets. Went to the staff to make sure and found that they had already gone. Very annoying as ought to be given early warning of impending moves. General Staff and Q branch moved into BOURECQ. Two motorcyclists dept at their billet. Continued the brigade line to BOURECQ and ran a new D5 cable line down main road to join Z R C air line. Completed by 5.15 P M	

Army Form C. 2118.

WAR DIARY
or
INTELLIGENCE SUMMARY. 3 Signal Squadron

October 1915

(Erase heading not required.)

Instructions regarding War Diaries and Intelligence Summaries are contained in F. S. Regs, Part II. and the Staff Manual respectively. Title pages will be prepared in manuscript.

Place	Date	Hour	Summary of Events and Information	Remarks and references to Appendices
BOURECQ	12th		Moved office into Bourecq closing for good at 10 A.M. Unfortunately our cable loop to the 2 A.C. Div. was faulty and owing to this, V.13.R. was "dis" from Z.R.C. for an hour and a half while same was being traced. Rude message received from Sigs V13R. General Staff, Q Branch, A.D.M.S. billeted here, other headquarter troops and details in ST HILAIRE. Motorcyclists collected three times a day and delivered three other times also. No other movements of troops.	
	13th		Lt. D.R.T. HALLIDAY 11th Hussars joined for duty with two servants and three horses. Gave machine gun officer of 6th Tank Bde three miles of German wire. He had been given some telephone wire - no wire.	
	14th		S.R.114 & No 4 C.F.N. moved into BOURECQ and we had to rearrange our billets slightly. Kept reading practice at 5.15. Slight fog interfered with good reading.	

1577 Wt. W10791/1773 500,000 1/15 D. D. & L. A.D.S.S./Forms/C. 2118.

WAR DIARY
INTELLIGENCE SUMMARY. 3 Signal Squadron

October 1915

Place	Date	Hour	Summary of Events and Information	Remarks and references to Appendices
BOURECQ	15 Oct 16		Cable laying parties for Lt Holliday with the trailer.	
	16th		VBR came off the line to 2RC without either of them notifying me and sent out a lineman to help him get through and then discovered that he had gone for good as there I came in as terminal to VC – 2RC – AAR line. At 11 am 2RC closed down at Allouagne and then I came in as terminal station on VC – AAR – 2C line. Reeled up the spare D5 cable line rendered spare by becoming terminal instead of intermediate. A large influx of infantry into the village and flooded us out of our billets. Some regiments of 21st Bde 7th Division come back to rest.	
	18th		At 9.30 am learnt that Headquarters were moving to FROGES at 3 pm. They left and also all the details from ST HILAIRE. Lt Fairclough took both cars and all the wire apps and commenced a line from Fruges to Bomy. Line was a few hundred yards short of VAR office in Bomy trailer and party were back by 4.30 having laid about 6½ miles of wire. Lt Holliday and a small party opened an office in Fruges at 3 pm.	

WAR DIARY
or INTELLIGENCE SUMMARY

Army Form C. 2118

3 Signal Squadron

October 1915

Place	Date	Hour	Summary of Events and Information	Remarks and references to Appendices
BOURECQ	1/10		Orders were issued for troops of division to move back on 19th. the date was then changed to 21st and about 8 p.m. was again altered for 19th. This entailed a lot of work for DR's between Bourecq and Fruges. A great deal of trouble was also caused by the Corps wireless in sending messages for V.C. at Fruges to V.C. at Bourecq and expecting them delivered. Much interruption on the line between VCR and APR and at one time wires and cam onto the line and we got all their signals. The French closed themselves and the Frenchmen found out nothing. I was able to give brigade notification of the impending move for the 19th and so they got a clear extra two hours notice as the DR from Fruges did not get in to VCR until about 10 P.M. There was a great rush of work in the office between 8.30 and 11 PM and then it ceased all night. Z Co moved to 20 MBRFS at noon leaving R2Co at Theronanne.	
	10th	At 9 am closed VCR at Bourecq. Completed Fruges - Bourecq line and arranged with VA to transfer my work to Z Co over their line. Lent them two operators. Worked to 6th Lev. Bde at Febvin-Palfart by leaving an orderly in the civil office at Flechin. also to New Bde H.Q. until the Fauquembergues.	

Army Form C. 2118

WAR DIARY
or
INTELLIGENCE SUMMARY

3 Signal Squadron

October 1915

Instructions regarding War Diaries and Intelligence Summaries are contained in F.S. Regs., Part II. and the Staff Manual respectively. Title Pages will be prepared in manuscript.

Place	Date	Hour	Summary of Events and Information	Remarks and references to Appendices
FRUGES	19th		Lt Fairbrugh reeled up all the cable from Bruay towards Pernes and was greatly delayed by the troops moving along the road on which he was working.	
	20th		At 8.30 am took over W office at Bony Castre with 2 operators and 2 linemen. Worked wheats to RZ CO along a line D1 line to F. the Blanche thence on line to Theronanne. In the morning was able to work through direct to the regiments week from NZ CO and we transmitted one to Bony. Fixed the 6" Bde offe the line from Beaumetz-les-Aire to Holliday hut — the line was strong by 4.30 P.M. Our corps commenced building an air line three shuwl from 1UWBSG. We built the line in Bruay Fruges into DS to our office. Lt Fairbrugh commenced taking down and reeling up the line from Wandonne towards Fauquembergues. Scot Car Rolls moved into Bony.	
	21st		7th Can Rde rejoined from 1st Army and took up two old ground at Fauquembergues. They kept men in and telephone office worked via PH who transmitted.	

WAR DIARY or INTELLIGENCE SUMMARY

Army Form C. 2118

Place	Date	Hour	Summary of Events and Information	Remarks and references to Appendices
FRUGES	21st		Improved and poled up the D.F. line. Cow Corps completed their through line and we took it into use with horse at 6.30 PM. Billets as usual. Headquarters troops with FRUGES 3 Field Squadron LUGY	
			4th Bde R.H.A. FRUGES Ammunition Column HEZECQUES	
			6th Cav Bde Ammunition Park AUCHEL	
			7th Cav Bde FEBVIN - RAZ-FAAT Supply Column LIKLERS	
			Brit Cav Bde PAUQUEM REROUES	
			ROMY	
	22nd		At Fauitstough commenced building a C.I. wire to Fauguembergues. Took over a drum of D. to VI. in exchange for their Civic Army Station Blende which I handed over to PH who had a requirement at ENGUN. Moved our office at Romy into the civil telephone office. Cut out the line B2CO or Police Blende opposite the upper left continuing line to P.G.	
	23rd		2CO second line finished but a contact on the line was worked more with at water for telephone. Continuing line to P.G.	
	24th		Took second Cav Corps line into use. wireman out removed things so one of the lines was showing many degrees of earth.	

WAR DIARY
or
INTELLIGENCE SUMMARY

Army Form C. 2118

3 Signal Squadron

October 1915

Place	Date	Hour	Summary of Events and Information	Remarks and references to Appendices
FRÜGES	24th		Received the Headquarters lorry which took all the men and single poles and wire from the line Fauquembergues – Inchiencourt which party took down. Completed the line temporarily with D3 cable. Rebuilt it for us in the town and we left cable laying on general Fork line until we got at 4.30 p.m. Withdrew party from Bomy. Supply column, Ammunition Park moved to LUMBRES.	
	25th		Completed air line into Fauquembergues. Quickly after breakdowns every line was down for a short time as the result of heavy rain and wind during the night. Most transmitters working to ear each owning otherwise to a faulty instrument.	
	26th		Ruled up D3 cable at Fauquembergues.	
	27th		L/Cpl Holliday commenced building a 6.1. wire trunk buzz & phone to cable train to PF & PK. Finished at buzzer at 3 p.m. Lt Cuthbyn out with buzzers to improve the existing cable lines. A course of telephony was started at Car Corps. Arrangements were made by General Staff and I was now taken into consultation at all times as Signal expert – I should have all questions of signal training referred to me.	

WAR DIARY

Army Form C. 2118

INTELLIGENCE SUMMARY — 3 Signal Squadron

Month: October 1915

Place	Date	Hour	Summary of Events and Information	Remarks and references to Appendices
FRU G.P.S.	28th		Lt Faithfulrye continuing line to P.H. Recalled him at 11.30 am as there was an icy wet wind blowing and showers of rain. The men were wet, chilled and in need of rum was greatly appreciated. Line was out from 7.30 am to 5.30 P.M. the line had been faulted at railway crossing to a high tree which swaying in the gale continually broke the wire. Linesmen asked for assistance and Lt Halliday went out to help.	
	29th		Lt Halliday continuing the P.H. line. Work stopped at 11 pm on stock of wire finished. Newburn for Cavalry into barns. 3 officers and 6 men. Captain E. P. Brocklehurst (Sigs P.G.S.) attending as supernumerary. Roughs some chickens and oaks from the gas works and attempts to improve the standings of the stable. Drains dug out. An open shed covered all the horses but no sides to keep out the wind or rain.	
	30th		Lt Halliday completed air-line through hedge with D.I. formed cable to air line at far end and reeled up the cable back to the signal office.	

WAR DIARY
or
INTELLIGENCE SUMMARY
(Erase heading not required.)

Army Form C. 2118

3 Signal Squadron
Oct/Nov 1915

Place	Date	Hour	Summary of Events and Information	Remarks and references to Appendices
FRUGES	30		During the month the sex mined signallers have not been attached to form from regiments joined. They were trained men thanks to the kindness of the adjutants. Names were called for of men deserving french decorations. No 28740 Sgt Shaw was recommended for the medaille militaire for conspicuous good work as an N.C.O. in charge of motorcyclists and for prompt delivery of all messages under varying conditions of weather and fire.	
	31		A last place arrange near P.G. office at Fauquembergues and they agreed to let on his tc Z.C.O. in the event of a "show" occurring. Much rain during the day and a very cold wind. Establishment of visual signallers was raised from 6 to 12, and one man joined mounted from each of the regular regiments in the division. Four of them were trained men.	

C Atkinson Lt OC
3 Signal Squadron RE

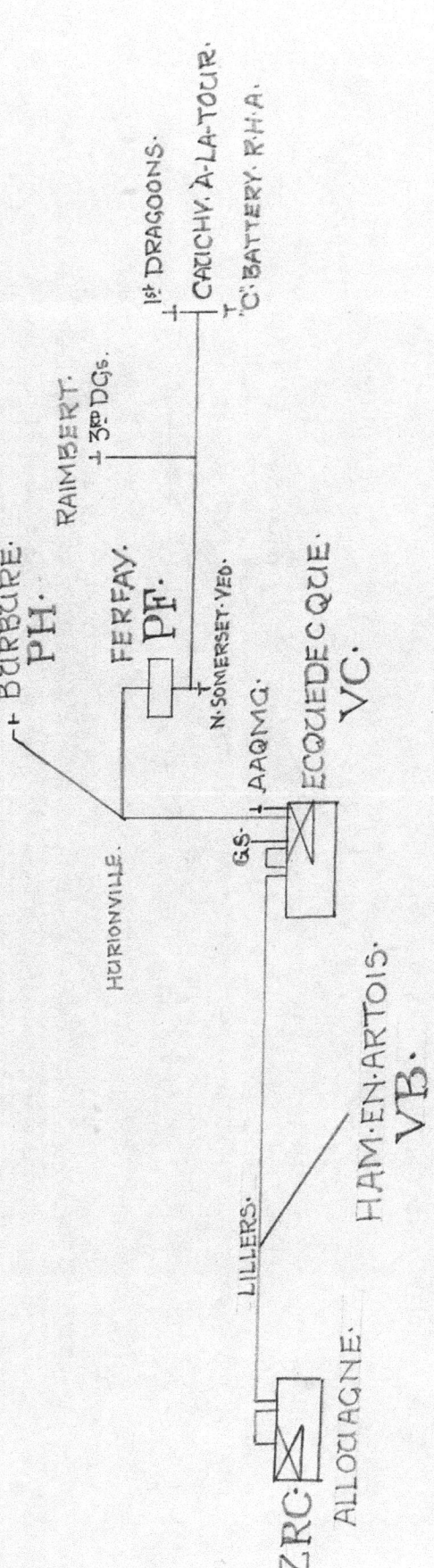

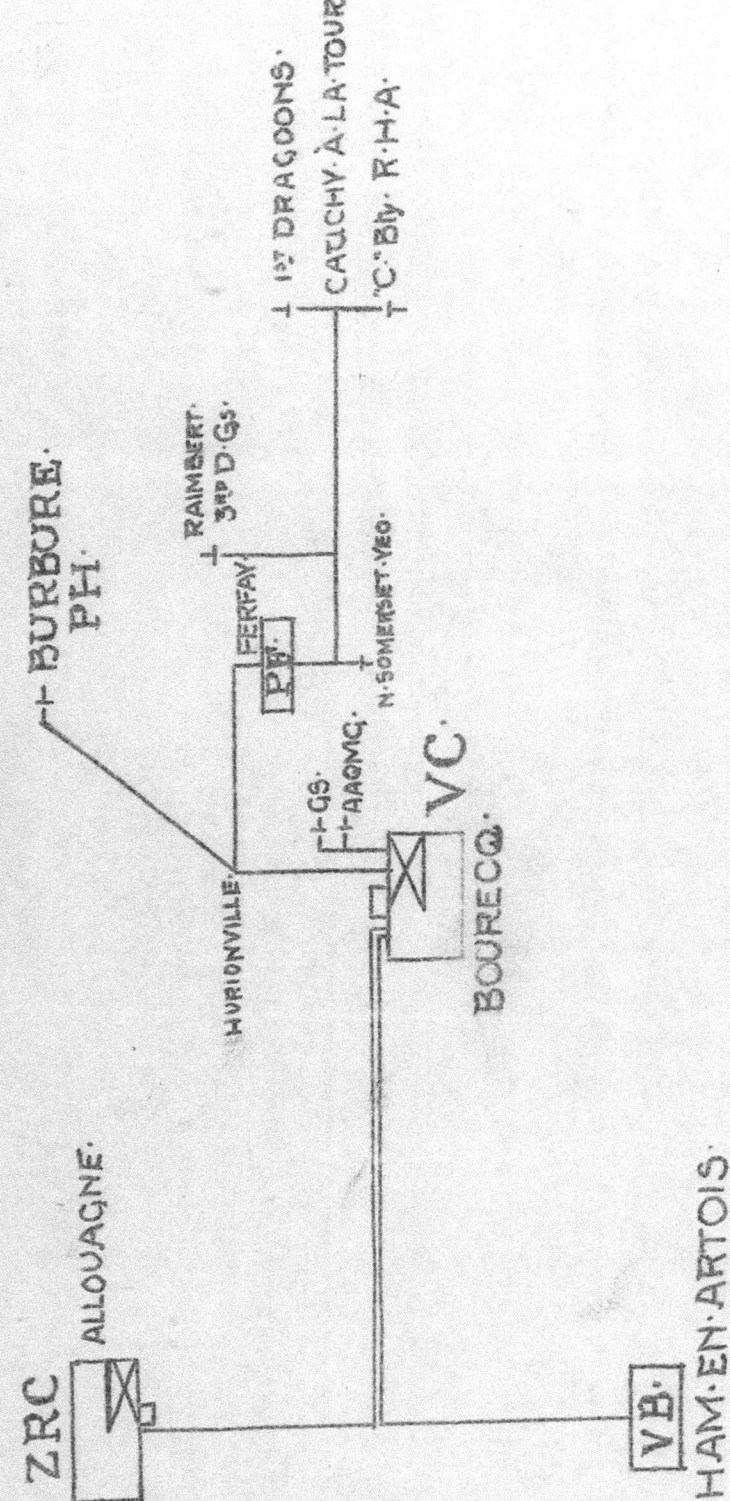

CIRCUIT DIAGRAM. 3RD SIGNAL SQUADRON.
OCTOBER 19. 1915.

CIRCUIT DIAGRAM. 3RD SIGNAL SQUADRON. OCTOBER 17. 1915.

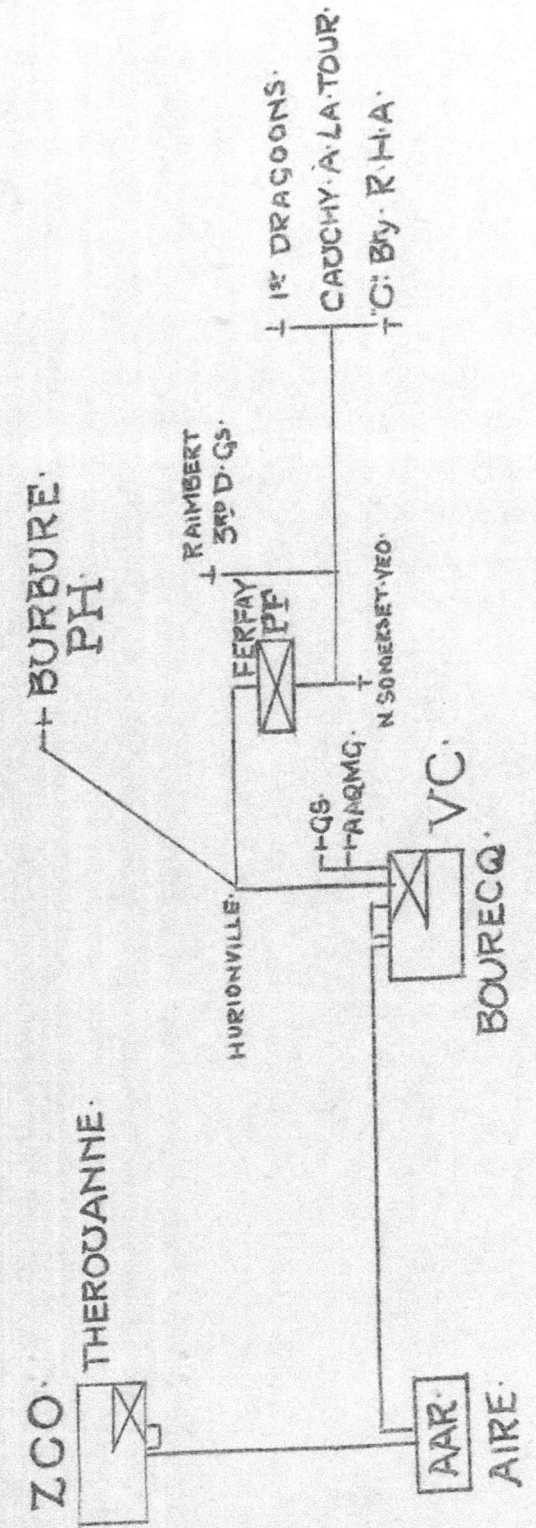

Nov. 1915

3rd Cavalry Division

3 Signal Sqn

WAR DIARY or INTELLIGENCE SUMMARY

Army Form C. 2118

November 1915.   3 Signal Squadron

Place	Date	Hour	Summary of Events and Information	Remarks and references to Appendices
FRUGES	1st		Ran out a D1 line to 6.3 Field Squadron at LUGY. Put in a bell ringing telephone. Bell rang to commence with, but into the heavy rain that fell during the day, this ceased and line could not be taken into use.	
	2nd		Advanced digging parties moved up — 6th Cav Bde } SERCUS 3 Field Squadron } 7 Cav Bde LYNDE. 8th Cav Bde } WALLON-CAPPEL 8th C.F.A. } Arrangements made for wires to be sent via 2CO, GHQ to HK office in Hazebrouck thence by motor cycle. One motor cyclist also attached to 3 F.S. in SERCUS to collect from parties at 10 AM and 4 PM. A motor cyclist sent daily from FRUGES at NOON to deliver to SERCUS and come back via ST OMER to bring the Times from the O.B. Section for compilation of Intelligence Summary.	
	3rd		Heavy rain and wind of last three days had caused many of the lines to break on PG line. Insulators were found to swing bats which swayed greatly in the wind.	

WAR DIARY
or
INTELLIGENCE SUMMARY 3 Signal Squadron

Army Form C. 2118

No. 1
Nov 1915

(Erase heading not required.)

Place	Date	Hour	Summary of Events and Information	Remarks and references to Appendices
FRUGES	3rd		Night had been fine. 3 F.S. line tested only 45 0 earth. Shuttleworth worked down it and with the aid of the sun reduced this to 18.0. The cold turns the ring quite easily and the indicator dropped satisfactorily on the exchange.	
	4th		Continuing line to P.H.	
	5th		Visual Scheme as attacked. Work stopped owing to rain and sport. Staff Ride, Director at Metringhem, translator Drucks at Sercies and Journay. Three motorcyclists with them and line with the Director. Willoder made visual arrangements to Sercies. Lasted till 2.30 P.M.	
	6th		Cut poles for comic air-line in HEZECQUES wood	
	7th		Continuing line to P.H.	
	8th		Captain Simon 3 Field Squadron placed in charge of a party at SEMPY and arrangements made to send to him twice weekly on Tuesday and Friday.	
	9th		Traube seen by General Fowler D.A.S. or Cavalry Corps. Yr. was raining and he did not see it working but although no opinion passed or gathered that he was not in favour of innovation like it	

WAR DIARY or INTELLIGENCE SUMMARY

Army Form C-2118

3 Signal Squadron

November 1915.

Place	Date	Hour	Summary of Events and Information	Remarks and references to Appendices
FRUGES	9th		Mr Halliday completed line to PH.	
	10		A digging party went up to work under 9th Corps. A line from 14K office Hazebrouck to WALLON CAPPEL given to us. Halliday took up an operator and fixed up line and telephone there. We then undertook on repairs order from Hazebrouck. Pulled up cable from Beaurreley to Bony using to trouble behind the half of the dumbed wagon as no can was available. Halting up to 5th Corps to arrange for communication for different parties. 50 rat of Pole in 29/ H14 a 4.2 delivering to to Party. Killed in huts in H14 a 6.0 Sheet 28.	
	11		Shipwith built air line through huge cornplace Dicable. Rain and blew during night in consequence a break on our lines line and two on PH, PF line.	
	13th		VCR at W Allen Cappel increased to two motorcyclists and one operator, allied the direction of 2 CO an line air Fauquemberquea in order to avoid crossing the railway by a big tree when surveying had in a mind was the cause of the break. Working party down PH line as the tri-drays had broken in many places when line zigzagged up an avenue of trees, ultimately from a big tree on to a little one	

WAR DIARY
or
INTELLIGENCE SUMMARY 3 Signal Squadron

November 1915

Army Form C. 2118

Instructions regarding War Diaries and Intelligence Summaries are contained in F.S. Regs., Part II. and the Staff Manual respectively. Title Pages will be prepared in manuscript.

(Erase heading not required.)

Place	Date	Hour	Summary of Events and Information	Remarks and references to Appendices
FRUGES	14th		Result of D.A.S. visit to Corps was that he placed an embargo on the issue of any more stores to the cavalry, so we have got to carry on as best we can though distances between billets area are so great regularly. Those last night. Built a D5 and D3 line from office to ROYON on party skirting either end and meeting in CREVY but completed 5.30 pm. We had the overhauls as it was full out so work was slow as wire beginning work alteration and lines had been so torn as to overhaul it. Prospected country towards HUCQUELIER and QUILEN where PB & PH were going to move to respectively. Improved and tested ROYON line. Heavy snow during the night. At 6.20 am motorcyclist arrived to get up the hill out of FRUGES. Dispatches from Corps Cyclist were	
	15th			
	16th		by car. Brother Bell moved to HUCQUELIER and started taking down the P6 line with two smaller parties and building it up in the new direction with another line relax in by 1.30 pm and as Brook tried to halfway through COUPELLE VIEILLE	

WAR DIARY
or
INTELLIGENCE SUMMARY 3 Signal Squadron

November 1915.

Army Form C.2118

(Erase heading not required.)

Instructions regarding War Diaries and Intelligence Summaries are contained in F. S. Regs., Part II. and the Staff Manual respectively. Title Pages will be prepared in manuscript.

Place	Date	Hour	Summary of Events and Information	Remarks and references to Appendices
FRUGES	16th		Arranged communication with civil post office at FRUGES from whom we could communicate with Railhead at MARESQUEL at HUCQUELIERS and to Supply Column at BEAURAINVILLE. Speaking very bad to MARESQUEL and the line was very noisy with the greatest difficulty that these showmessages could be received.	Pl. 7 Gentral
	17th		Reorganised radio headquarters every night before fair. 6 Cow Roll moved to ROYON. 3 Field Squadron moved to COUPELLE NEUVE. Ammunition Column to COUPELLE VIEILLE. Ammunition Park to FRUGES. Ammunition Horse Transport to FRUGES. Sear working party out in headquarters lorry to complete PC line. Sent a party to cut pives in HECQUES wood. The building party were greatly delayed by numerous short of nails and having to wait for them. We were short of mandates too and had to take them down off the old PC line which was other work as they were better insulated and great ingenuity was required to now and the nails without breaking the insulators.	

WAR DIARY or INTELLIGENCE SUMMARY

Army Form C 2118

3 Signal Squadron

November 1915

Place	Date	Hour	Summary of Events and Information	Remarks and references to Appendices
FRUGES	17		Another party completed the line into the 6th Bn HQ in new office this would have been finished tonight if full supplies of stores had been forthcoming. Can Corps Signals kindly helped us by lending us our line from HUCQUELIERS through QUILEN to road junction 1 mile W. of BELLEVUE Sheet ARRAS 7. At 4.30 a very heavy storm of sleet impeded work and the party returned home leaving about 600 yards remaining to be done.	
	18		Line completed at 11.30 am working and speaking satisfactory. Another Bde Headquarters party have since moved definitely but some units moved. They had a trunk office PHR in QUILEN. reps. a pair of trainers and some men with PHR for this maintenance. A party working up from this end to improve long stay and remove earths. 69 & Barailly Brigade came in on an Bway line and went out to investigate. They had moved into LAIRES and were using our old PF line for FERVIN-PALFART respectively. Arranged to leave it up for them but to cut communication into PH his at junction LAIRES - BEAUMETZ-LES-MIRES.	

WAR DIARY or INTELLIGENCE SUMMARY

3 Signal Squadron

November 1915

Army Form C. 2118

Place	Date	Hour	Summary of Events and Information	Remarks and references to Appendices
FRUGES	19th		Day off for the men. Gen. PG sent the exchange and the 2nd ADC to Commander in chief sends to the 2nd Life Guards which was a great achievement. (STONER to HUCQUELIERS)	
	20th		LT HALLIDAY took over temporary command of the 4 th Signal Troop vice CAPT HERAMS appointed Staff Captain to 7 th Cav. Bde. Picked up line to LUGY and from Beauval-les-Aires to LAIRES	
	22nd		Conference at the General Staff on dismounted organization to be this division were ordered to provide a brigade of three battalions of three companies.	
	23–28th		Buzzing and lamp reading practice where men could see his own light and how necessary it was for him to send his dots slowly so as to give the filament time to date slowly so as to give the filament time to	
	29th		8 Cavalry Brigade moved from BOMY to QUIEN. 10 th Hussars to HUMBERT RHG to be BELLE VUE allowed time to the one on PG – PH line which was running near their door.	
	30th		Rolled up the line to BOMY.	

Dec. 1915

3rd Signal Sqn.
See
Vol XI

3 C D

WAR DIARY or INTELLIGENCE SUMMARY

Army Form C. 2118

3 Signal Squadron

December

Place	Date	Hour	Summary of Events and Information	Remarks and references to Appendices
Dec 1st FRUGES			Tour of the fortnightly medical inspection took place. VERMELLES-HULLUCH built a line to 3 Field gun Mtrs and Office w/ COUPELLE NEUVE	
FRUGES	Dec 2nd		Picked up cable line from FEBVIN-PAL-FART to LAIRES also a length of D1 left behind by 6th and some more left by Indns & some linemen walked back half of our men stranded on ZCO line tightening stays and driving in pegs. Raining nearly lead all the morning. Speaking very bad to 7 CLS.	
	4th		Walked remainder of ZCO line and removed all carts off PH line.	
	5th		Got drum of galvanized iron wire from 2nd Can Div.	
	6th		Smoke helmet inspection and lecture by Captain Young R.A.M.C. on Gas smoke helmet use and adjustment.	
	7th		Took 10 men to FMBRY where a gas expert from C.149 gave us a short lecture on the helmets and then we put them on and walked into a gas filled tunnel. Helmets perfectly efficient. All worked	
	8th		FMATLOUGH commenced building iron wire line to Pte Picket at all wavelets and north of BRBony and tapping line Regimental lines. They stopped work just short of CAEOUY being short of materials.	
	9th		Held a conference with Brigade and Regimental signal officers to decide questions on training scheme and to decide number of men signalling schools to be used to write.	

WAR DIARY or INTELLIGENCE SUMMARY

Army Form C. 2118

Seventh **3 Signal Groshow**
1915

Place	Date	Hour	Summary of Events and Information	Remarks and references to Appendices
PROGES	10th		Railhead changed to MONTREUIL. Went down to see if I could meet a Stephens for his R.T.O. An officer from Line of Communication Company turned up to do the same thing. He had no wire so I assisted him. Got a subalterns line from civil office Pho 42. Supply Column No 35.	
	11th		Party out on P14 – P6 line to improve and also to improve and walking very slow and tedious.	Raining hard and walking very wet
			Capt. SIMON and party from SEMPY moved into PHILIBERTE Farm which had been vacated by the R.H.Q. who moved headquarters to AIX-EN-ISSART.	
	12th		Several Signar cars came up to replace casualty. Visited VCR at WAILLONCAPPEL. Picked up one of our returning DR's wife had broken down at WAMDONNE and shortly after the steering gear gave way and we ran into the nearest tree. Front axle broke and off side near bent. Car had only been overhauled on 2nd [mist?] and [mission?] steering arm was missing and no remains of a splitpin. None of the glass broken. NOT a good can as the [?] would not go in except with a jerk and not altogether.	
	13th		Picked up cable as far as Gregory. H Faurtheugh to Hesdin and made inquiries regarding land telephonic communication to Montreuil	
	14th		Reports [?] to French authorities at ST POL and they put in night at one of [?] Obtained permission for the French telegraph office to accept Requested and obtained permission for the French telegraph office to accept censored letters in English. Ammunition Park work steps made one to others of VB's D1 winder hard.	

1875 Wt. W 593/826 1,000,000 4/15 J.B.C. & A. A.D.S.S./Forms/C. 2118.

WAR DIARY or INTELLIGENCE SUMMARY

December 1915   3 Signal Squadron

Army Form C. 2118

Place	Date	Hour	Summary of Events and Information	Remarks and references to Appendices
FRUGES	14th		Sent to Walter Cappel reported back to replace D1 wire by DS and improved set wire generally.	
	15		Lt SCOTT of Royals and Lt JAMES of R.H.G. came for a 5 days course writing, lamp reading practice indoors. Brigr. & Colns. kept reading medical inspection of men and billets. Officers doing Superintendence fortnightly and exchange of units.	
	16		L/C CAPP, Pte GOOCH Signallers examined and passed by Cavalry Corps for Proficiency Pay.	
	17			
	18		One man of each regiment in the division sent for a month's course with wr. Regtl. Sunday only spare hour. A good examination in hygiene.	
	19		Time table for class as follows: 8.30 – 9 am B class bugging – 12.30 A 10.30 – 12.30 A — bugging returns 2 – 4.30 B 5.30 – 6.30 M + B lecture on instruments, electricity and magnetism 5.15 – 6.15 Officers separate lecture on internal economy communications	9 – 10.30 A class visual signalling B class line work
	21		Staff Ride. Direction with 4 motorcycles via SAINS-LES-FRESSIN Monastier Direct had four at cross-roads W of RUCHMPS and Blue Force in ROYON Chateau, ride finished each with three motor-cyclists. Ride finished at 3 pm.	

WAR DIARY or INTELLIGENCE SUMMARY

Army Form C. 2118

3 Signal Squadron

December 1915.

Instructions regarding War Diaries and Intelligence Summaries are contained in F.S. Regs., Part II. and the Staff Manual respectively. Title Pages will be prepared in manuscript.

(Erase heading not required.)

Place	Date	Hour	Summary of Events and Information	Remarks and references to Appendices
FROGES	23rd		Lt HALLIDAY returned from commanding 4th Signal Troop	
	24th		New Singer van issued to replace one lost by Highland Contingent on & 11th regiment & Brigade	
	25th		Christmas Day. Reduced strength of office only, an early post to Brigade and only received early post from Cavalry Corps. Closed completely from 12–2 P.M. During those hours we held a Squadron dinner in the Hotel du Commerce which was a great success.	
	26th		Complaints received that buzzer signals from 8th Cav Bde to us had been heard in the Saint Omer civil exchange. Investigated and traced fault.	
			Holiday given to class for these two days.	
	27th		Orders received that Dismounted Division was to form, fortnights, some of equipment for battalion issued to them and remainder came during the day. As follows: — 7 D3 telephones, 8 miles D1 wire, 8 plains & bells linemen, 2 cookstoves, 2 curvier. leans, 2 tins tape/ buzzer exchange, five lanterns but falling 100 yds of oxygen. 16 drums D1	
	28th		Men for Brigade section paraded at PT. ST MICHEL and were inspected. L/c Capps Dr Mitchell Dr Hunt Dr Lampard Junr G.S. waggon and 6 horse team Slopen Cpl Rundlett Dr Ponter	
	29th		Proceeded to LUMBRES to join the Signal Company	
	30th		Running and campfire indoors.	
	31st		Lt Southbergh Cpl Clements & Kindly with 3rd hiker and pair of horses entrained Sgt Procter Dr Tanwell Dr Congleton at MARESQUEL for duty with 3rd Dismounted Brigade Signal Section	

A.Chute Lt O/c
3rd Signal Squadron

3c

3 Signal Sq
Jan 1916
Vol XII

Army Form C. 2118

WAR DIARY
or
INTELLIGENCE SUMMARY

3 Signal Squadron

January 1916

(Erase heading not required.)

Place	Date	Hour	Summary of Events and Information	Remarks and references to Appendices
FROGES	1st		Dismounted Brigade tested lift for duty travelling by train to BETHUNE. Visual signal practice	
	2nd		M/Cpl E.A. Hellmutt awarded the D.C.M. Lte SKIPWITH Sr J. WHYTE Lte C. HARDY Cpl E.V. SMITH } mentioned in Sir John French's dispatches.	
	4		Lt Halliday come air line from Rryon to replace cable.	
	5		Cpl WHITEHEAD to cadets school St Omer with a view to obtaining a commission. Re staying Corr Corps line. Built air line to 6 C.F.A. billeted in the town	
	6		Lecture on signal work.	
	7			
	8		Lt HALLIDAY left to join Dismounted Signal Coy COY at SAILLY	
	10		Sgt Jamie carrying on the building of air line from P.F. Sr Ireland, Southurst P to Gooch Saunders by train to LOMBRES to join the Brigade Signal Section.	
	11		S'Cayeris Corr Corps line.	

WAR DIARY or INTELLIGENCE SUMMARY

Army Form C. 2118

Instructions regarding War Diaries and Intelligence Summaries are contained in F.S. Regs., Part II and the Staff Manual respectively. Title Pages will be prepared in manuscript.

(Erase heading not required.)

Place	Date	Hour	Summary of Events and Information	Remarks and references to Appendices
FRUGES	12th		Cavalry Corps sent a party to change their line where it runs near Le Bois de Fruges. The 2nd Battalion air dragging it sunk entanglement and his and stays interfering with the work. Relaid about 3 miles bringing it in closer to the road.	
	13th		Cut down more poles from the HEZECQUES wood.	
	14th		Picked up 2 miles of copper wire that cuts had left behind.	
	Thu		Cut some more poles	
	15		Put PF through into the air line and cleared earths to where many down.	
	19		Picked up cable from Pay on to Cagny.	
	24		L/C. Hurrell on his motor bicycle received on honour at 1/C dismounted Signals in Brooks Keeper	
	25		Sgt Chance sent to Cavalry Signals Temporary CAPTAIN from 1/10/15 to re-is in LT C SKIPWITH Mounted	
	26		Command of the Squadron	
	28		1st Halliday returned from the Dismounted Division Signals. Staging full Squadron line.	
	29,30		Laid 14 miles of new wire and indicators for to augment hosts. Lt Halliday continues PF air line	

C.H. ...... Capt.
3 Signal Squadron

WAR DIARY
or
INTELLIGENCE SUMMARY 3 Signal Squadron

February 1916

Army Form C. 2118

Place	Date	Hour	Summary of Events and Information	Remarks and references to Appendices
FRUGES	Feb 3rd		Obtained a twenty-line test board from 2co and fitted it in the office and re-wired to suit, with D3 cable to replace the bell wire in use before.	
	4th		Lt Halliday assumed temporary command of the squadron whilst Capt Skipwith was attached to Dismounted Division Signals.	
	6th	10	Staying and improving Brigade lines.	
	11th		3rd Dismounted Brigade were relieved by the 36th Infantry Brigade and returned to billets in FRUGES area. Only casualty that occurred was owing to one man running helter from a tin onto a brazier and setting himself on fire. G. Failing, and temporary command of squadron.	
	16th		Storm with considerable snow storm. Damage on G.H. lines and needed party to repair it.	
	17		Revised the system of clerking in the office and made the Supervisor keep the telegraph register which had normally been kept together with the messages by the operators in the telegraph room. 2co has patrolled the whole length on foot.	

Average of messages for week ending Feb 5.

	Incoming	Outgoing	Transmitted	Total
Average	162	149	77	388.
Daily highest	209	196	110	460.

WAR DIARY or **INTELLIGENCE SUMMARY**

Army Form C. 2118

February 1916. 3 Signal Squadron

(Erase heading not required.)

Instructions regarding War Diaries and Intelligence Summaries are contained in F.S. Regs., Part II. and the Staff Manual respectively. Title Pages will be prepared in manuscript.

Place	Date	Hour	Summary of Events and Information	Remarks and references to Appendices
			Average of messages for week ending Feb 14th	
			Outgoing Incoming Total	
			Highest daily 286 166 —	
			Average 206 146 426	
			Messages for week ending Feb 21	
			Highest daily 250 212 —	
			Average 212 168 342	
			Messages for week ending Feb 29	
			Highest daily — — 460	
			Average — — 480	
Huys	21		Received the previous class of training. 1 man came from own regiment and two officers from the division. Lt Fairtlough assumed command in Capt Shipside on leave.	
	22-29		Class work. Duties and his maintenance. Brigrs known manny	

O.H. [signature]

Army Form C. 2118

WAR DIARY
or
INTELLIGENCE SUMMARY 3 Signal Squadron
(Erase heading not required.)

Month 1916.

Instructions regarding War Diaries and Intelligence Summaries are contained in F. S. Regs., Part II. and the Staff Manual respectively. Title Pages will be prepared in manuscript.

Place	Date	Hour	Summary of Events and Information	Remarks and references to Appendices
FRUGES	1st		Capt. Shepherd returned, [?] of the situation on returning from leave. Principal Staff Office. No officers attended.	
	2nd		Wire unrolled [?]. 2nd Cav. Div. would very likely exchange areas into the 1st Cav. Div. and no arrangements were made for handing over the communication centres on this [?].	
	3		Sgt. Menzies joined from 3rd Signal Troop as Sergeant Major, and Sgt. Garner posted to that Troop. Examined the class of instruction after having given them a few examination papers.	
	5-7		Fairly heavy falls of snow which did some damage to the lines.	
	12		Assembled a class of 12 men, one from each regiment and battery, also 2 officers 2/Lt. Clery 3 D.G.'s & Lt. Henry [?] Yeomanry. Built a D5 line into class & [?] station where the G.O.C. is establishing a Divisional School of Instruction. Complete by 1.30 PM building both ways.	
	16		Col. Rolly of the French War Office came and inspected our office. Wired up our R.E. waggon lorries & a visual signal station. Mounted the two Glease is input to 6th Signal Troop.	

1875 Wt. W593/826 1,000,000 4/15 J.B.C. & A.   A.D.S.S./Forms/C. 2118.

WAR DIARY
or
INTELLIGENCE SUMMARY

Army Form C. 2118

3 Signal Squadron

March 1916

Place	Date	Hour	Summary of Events and Information	Remarks and references to Appendices
FRUGES	17th		Checked by Col George for the non fitting of our collars. Some further interspersion even since formation had changed. We were instructed and we were allowed to indent for fresh ones. Great collar harness.	
			Marching order parade followed by a minute inspection of each man. Major Page - G.S.O.2 inspected the squadron in marching order that afternoon. Only criticisms were that the M.O. was not at all out on parade, that in one or two cases the men's rifles were not easy to draw, and of course the fitting of our collars.	
	18th		Waggons & teams out to exercise in draught. Troop drill and jumping with the mounted men.	
	19th		Cpl Wright - evacuated an being of unsuitable trade & Cpl Capps mounted in his place and placed in charge of the stables.	
	20th		Half of the class built an iron wire line for 6th Bde down as Beauvonnelle, the other half built a D3 line from Ammunition Column at Coupelle Vieille on to G Battery RHA at Wailly. G. was an Pit cable not kept in trench otherwise we could telegraph to them.	
	21st		Picked up about 4 miles of cable from Trancourt château towards Blangy. Had been left there by the French.	

WAR DIARY or INTELLIGENCE SUMMARY

Army Form C. 2118

Place	Date	Hour	Summary of Events and Information	Remarks and references to Appendices
FROGES	21st		They were using some light bamboo poles with an ebonite insulator with a niche for wires for using with naked wires. Opened up a C.O's office in the store room so as to be always on the spot when wanted.	
	23rd		Commenced replacing D5 line to Tranecourt by iron wire and some wooden brackets nailed at intervals on to tree with a stay supporting each one above. Fairtlough's suggestion for line trans- built on lines so as to allow a certain amount of swaying without breaking the line or pulling off the bindings.	This Mr had to be
	24		Got back our 10 line German exchange from the Corps and both it in use as well as the other having about 14 people now on the 'phone. Fixed up Supply Column with a telephone borrowing a priva+e one from the Madame	

WAR DIARY
or
INTELLIGENCE SUMMARY

Army Form C. 2118

3 Signal Squadron

March 1916

Place	Date	Hour	Summary of Events and Information	Remarks and references to Appendices
FRUGES	24th		Heavy fall of snow in the evening accompanied by thunder and sleet was dis- to all three Brigades at 10 in the evening and in the car & van & put through with care but the firemen did not get back till 5 AM.	
	25th		Mr Halliday and men clears to repair the damage done on Pk Pl ho Mr Clery and Mr Henry returned to their regiments after a fortnights course.	
			Lt Spicer 1st Lifeguards W. Heyworth - Savage Royals L. Phelan "C" RHA arrived for course of instruction.	
	27th		A passing train stampeded the horses whilst watering. Three driving horses down but no harm done and all the horses retrieved bar knocked down but no harm done and all the horses retrieved bar did not come back to the stables on their own.	
	29th		Mr Faulthings made a useful chaff-cutter which was taken to use	
	30th		Have been under G.H.Q troops for some few days but made no difference will last say when they moved to Montreuil & therefore	

Army Form C. 2118

WAR DIARY
or
INTELLIGENCE SUMMARY
(Erase heading not required.)

March 1916

3 Signal Squadron RE

Instructions regarding War Diaries and Intelligence Summaries are contained in F.S. Regs., Part II. and the Staff Manual respectively. Title Pages will be prepared in manuscript.

Place	Date	Hour	Summary of Events and Information	Remarks and references to Appendices
FRUGES			Messages dealt with week ending	
			March 21st Average ——— 165 ——— 192 ——— 357	
			Highest ——— 202 ——— 220 ——— 378.	
			28th Average ——— 152 ——— 194 ——— 346	
			Highest ——— 167 ——— 211 ——— 378	
			Incoming Outgoing Total	

CHeywith Capt OC
3 Signal Squadron
31/3/16.

WAR DIARY
INTELLIGENCE SUMMARY

Army Form C. 2118

3 Signal Squadron R.E.

April 1916

Place	Date	Hour	Summary of Events and Information	Remarks and references to Appendices
FRUGES	1st		2 C.O. paraded stores and one building party and the class paraded a second and commenced building a pair of iron vices to stores. Started 7 AM and back by 3.45 PM and having used all available stores.	HESDIN P.K.
	2nd		Parade much for the house and waggons 9 AM to 2 PM. 2 Working parties, one yesterday, his class did not go line built in through town and took on to pair of iron wires at the Post Office. Line through by 3 PM this a very heavy swing on the line which was eventually traced to the iron standard at P.O. making contact and short circuit. Line working satisfactorily in more and more by 9 PM. Working now to 2 H.D. Army.	
	4th		Officer in telephone to Z.C.O. C.O. telephoned to the D.A.D.R.G.H.Q. troops who suddenly arrived in his intention to do a Ridio scheme but bring the fifths of series of fine sunny days, the sun did not "put" in an appearance. The scheme worked satisfactorily with flag and little cope except to one station who were too far and with whom touch could not be established. Stations P.K. 3 men PB 2 men PD 2 men and V.C. 9 men.	

WAR DIARY or INTELLIGENCE SUMMARY

Army Form C. 2118

April 1916

3 Signal Squadron

(Erase heading not required.)

Instructions regarding War Diaries and Intelligence Summaries are contained in F.S. Regs., Part II. and the Staff Manual respectively. Title Pages will be prepared in manuscript.

Place	Date	Hour	Summary of Events and Information	Remarks and references to Appendices
BRUCES	5th		Placed under Reserve Corps (2CO) at Wailly.	above hospital
			All Q correspondence continues to be sent to GHQ troops at Houdain	
	6th		Placed in communication with 2CO via HD in Ennemain	
			Visual scheme with PF in vicinity of Thinville and down to Roger valley. PF	PD. corner of Regigne wood
			Bellevue APF	PC. corner of wood disappearing down hill to Verdun
			Out 8.30 am	PB. on road opposite
			APF	VC
			IrwinD 1, 2 men	
			APH } 2 men cross roads to Thionville	
			VC 3 men	
			moved HQ up once from Back 3 pm	

WAR DIARY
INTELLIGENCE SUMMARY

3 Signal Squadron

April 1916

Army Form C. 2118

Place	Date	Hour	Summary of Events and Information	Remarks and references to Appendices
BRUGES	8th		Class dismissed on completion of this month's course. Visual scheme with all three brigades. General idea that each brigade were reconnoitering the crossings of the main Canal at Beauvainville Moule and Morel. Brigade headquarters and Divisional headquarters to move up as the country was reported clear. Good luck kept with P.H. and P.F. and though established with P.G. no messages were coming through from them.	

1st Phase

P.F. Mon de Torcy
APF — 2emede D.
P.H — APH — Henonville
P.G — MC.P.G
V.C — Bellure croisements

2nd Phase

APF hill above EMBRY
PH — APH
PG —
VC Henonville
CPG

WAR DIARY or INTELLIGENCE SUMMARY

Army Form C. 2118

3 Signal Squadron
April 1916

Place	Date	Hour	Summary of Events and Information	Remarks and references to Appendices
FRUGES	8th		Out 8.30 am and not back till 5.30 pm. Some delay caused by inability of telephone operators to reel up the line with the speed of himself, and good line practice obtained. All signallers not experienced at this with the long signals. New procedure seems to be pretty well understood.	
	10		Canadian Cavalry Brigade (PCA) joined the division. Continued the Transcourt line on to them. Line earthy so considerable trouble in ringing them till and they had to pay constant attention to it. Line through 2 pm.	
	11		Picked up about 8 miles of French copper cable from Blangy to Houvrines. Laid out a line of this French cable for PCA from Km. 64 on Blangy to Aubry-les-Hesdin. PCA provided the building party. Considerable delay caused by the difficulty in replacing the coils of cable on to No 4 collapsible wire drum. Line laid on by 5 pm. Raining all day. Cleared cuttes off PCA line. Tried to arrange for one wire chiv with a separate drop indicator for Transcourt Hill. Shelter did not work very well, and School experienced great difficulty in getting us. Eco rule up this line to Hesdin & we worked to them only this night.	

WAR DIARY or INTELLIGENCE SUMMARY

Army Form C. 2118

3 Signal Squadron

Month: April 1916

Place	Date	Hour	Summary of Events and Information	Remarks and references to Appendices
BRUGES	13		Kept PCA on magneto bell for ringing purposes with a switch to indicator for sending messages. Repaired and twine building.	
	14		Placed motorcyclists Burdett, Clements, French, Kelleher on duty as superintendents so as to release other N.C.O's for signalling training.	
	15		Riding and Troop drill for all mounted men. Built some jumps.	
	16		Marching order parade. Ag exits out under Sgt Preston. Horses and limbers out under O.C. Instituted friendly relations with the Canadian Signal Troop by allowing them to defeat us at football by 2-1 after a close game.	
	17		Replaced some copper air line on PCA line by galvanized as former was required by the Corps.	
	18		Buggery and "visual" lectures to signallers in morning. Telephone lectures in afternoon.	

WAR DIARY
INTELLIGENCE SUMMARY

April 1916.   3 Signal Squadron R.E.

Army Form C. 2118

Place	Date	Hour	Summary of Events and Information	Remarks and references to Appendices
FRUGES	19		Fortnightly medical inspection. Mounted drill & cable work.	
	20-21		Lecture on contours and map reading.	
	22		Mounted drill & cable work. Visual signalling. Pair work flags.	
	24-28		Route march. Mounted transport long work.	
	25 w 28			
	29		Pair of telephone wires run from the camp of N.S.Y. & 6 M.G.S. to the Torquet golf course onto pair of civil wires at villa LES PYROLES to Torquet. Communication through by 2.15 PM and speaking good to 10 but not 6 PF. Telephone number le Torquet zero 248. Transformer obtained and speaking then better on to civil line.	
	30			

Shepsuite W.O.
3 Signal Squadron

WAR DIARY
or
INTELLIGENCE SUMMARY

3 Signal Squadron

Army Form C. 2118

May 1916

Place	Date	Hour	Summary of Events and Information	Remarks and references to Appendices
FRUGES	2nd		Marching orders and visual signalling. R.H.Q. to Merlimont. Telephone communication to them via Rue & Etaples with improvised switching or similar plugs. Cable work with improvised cable cart. Visual signalling - bad work in transmitting, correctly figures and accompanying symbols	
	3rd			
	4th		Cable work. Lt Faulkingh went to Receive Coy for attachment to the Wireless to gain a little familiarity with the Inaugurated Summer Hours.	
	5th		Stables 5.45. Parade 6 a.m. Breakfast & duties. Parade 9 a.m. Stables 10.30 a.m. Parade 2 p.m. for work on visual signalling. Riding school. Bugging and lecture on visual a class of 12 men from all the C. Sq's assembled for a week's course of semaphore — a repeater course Riding school and jumping. Ground reconnaissance between HES.D.N — CAMPAGNE — SAUCHOY with a view to divisional scheme.	
	6th			
	9th		Tried to get a pigeon loft in the town for a little practice flying and to give the pigeon men some interest in them, then found and cleaned out a loft with a few birds and them but owner stuck as he said trop. he would have to kill any birds that we trained or he was not allowed to keep them	

WAR DIARY
or
INTELLIGENCE SUMMARY

(Erase heading not required.)

May 1916 — 3 Signal Squadron

Army Form C. 2118

Place	Date	Hour	Summary of Events and Information	Remarks and references to Appendices
BRUGES	10th		Saddlery and medical inspection. Route march practice two round the town and moving into the billets held into the older officers. Got as a subsidiary office where we could train superintendents, linemen and operators.	
	11th		Reserve lorries moved from WIZERNY to REGNIERE ECLUSE into signal office at BERNAY	
	12th		Marching order parade.	
	14th		Advance party V.R. started to MAISON PONTHIEU & headquarters emitting communications to suit our requirements, in training area	
	15th		Division moved into ST RIQUIER training area. The Brigade & Divisional Staffs commenced a staff ride on the way down. The G.O.C. wished to test our visual communications but it was raining and one could not see more than 1000 yards. Rendez-vous at Neuville near Campagne to khaki at 9 am. Dismissed at 11 & proceeded across country to MAISON PONTHIEU via Contreville, Hocteville, Neuilli Civil telephonic communication taken away, & Chateau St Pol thereon to W. We the former infantry the rest	

WAR DIARY or INTELLIGENCE SUMMARY

Army Form C. 2118

Place	Date	Hour	Summary of Events and Information	Remarks and references to Appendices
RANGES MAISON PONTHIEU	15th		Bugger line galvanized iron wire to YVRENCH where went to D14 at NOYELLES-EN-CHAUSSEE and to P1F at ST RIQUIER into the 12th Infantry Brigade lived on for the night at YVRENCH. PF transmitted for us to PG Bugger to BOIS L'ABBAYE and more in superimposed on telephone pair to ABBEVILLE. Sent then two operators and a lineman. 3rd Field Squadron went into camp at Paris Plage.	
	16th		VC remained open all through & Brigades opened up for it. In every four hours during the day. Left 17 men behind. Sent two DR's back to VC daily and also into M36 to meet the DR'S runner from GHQ and the dn. Cleared the civil line to Contents which was badly over hung with branches. Put in German exchange. Civil exchange not working so only plugged through there.	

WAR DIARY
or
INTELLIGENCE SUMMARY

Army Form C. 2118

May 1916

Signed Reginald Growden

Place	Date	Hour	Summary of Events and Information	Remarks and references to Appendices
BRUGES MAISON-PONTHIEU	16th		On D1 had in through the window. All available men reconnoitred the area of ground over which manoeuvres were taking place.	
	18th		Divisional exercise under the criticism of Reserve Corps commander Gen George Rushgram at FAIRMONT at 8.20 AM, where scheme commenced. Divisional Report Centre opened at Bois Granier, one by orderly & PH by motorcycle to PF by helio to PB & number later moved to hill 92 came to PC by helio PH by gallopers, PF by helio and motorcycle. Scheme closed about 2.30. Work was good except that find message sent to D14 went only by motorcycle instead of gallopers which delayed it somewhat.	
	20th		Divisional scheme with Gen Campbell as GOC and Genl Vaughan criticizing. Rendezvous 8 am at Yvrench. Scheme commenced 9 am report centre opened at Bois Granier.	

WAR DIARY or INTELLIGENCE SUMMARY

3 Signal Squadron

May 1916

Army Form C. 2118

Place	Date	Hour	Summary of Events and Information	Remarks and references to Appendices
MAISON-PONTHIEU	20th		Com to PF by helio to PG, PH by orderly. Later moved to Hill 92. O comm to PF by helio, to PH by orderly. Helio and to PG by galloper. Later moved to new where light railway crossing ST RIQUIER DOMVAST road. Hence Com by helio to PH, PF, PG, TA and a percent of all stations at once. Returned then work on send- and- receive with all its messages. 10.30 p Gallopers were sent-	
FRUGES	21st		Marched back to permanent billets at Fruges. 4th Rgl R.H.A. moved to St Riguier and Canadian Cavalry Brigade to Bois L'Abbaye. One operator and one linesman were left at St Riguier for assistance. + telephone + wires set kept on there. Divisional PCA line directing Transmount Chateau and hitched up the piece where it originally led in.	

Army Form C. 2118

WAR DIARY or INTELLIGENCE SUMMARY 3 Signal Squadron

May 1916

Place	Date	Hour	Summary of Events and Information	Remarks and references to Appendices
FRUGES	22.		D.R.L.S. rider from St Omer to Aubenté called at office all parcels for 3rd Brigade on way back delivering from them. Zco had built us a few huts but heading in to Frévent now and so we were able to put an exchange and work reprintposed to V.C.R. (Fruges) into V.C. (Frévent) intermediate to H.D. (Heuchin). The P.C.Paris terminates at V.C. & other half used for bigger line in to V.C.R. Arranged that work for the Field Squadron in camp at Paris Plage should go to Étaples where they worked inside for it twice a day.	to note
	23		3 D.Co's to camp at— Merlimont 16th Hussars —— 2nd Life Guards —— Merlimont Plage Permission could not be obtained from the Town Mayor at Merlimont, though they were driven for to le Touquet exchange to le Touquet exchange	

WAR DIARY or **INTELLIGENCE SUMMARY** 3 Signal Squadron

Army Form C. 2118

May 1916

Place	Date	Hour	Summary of Events and Information	Remarks and references to Appendices
FROGES	26		Proposals c/battery, 6 M.G.S moving to Frezni and Cenron. Sent a party to build from Frezni to valley. They knocked off work at 7.15 PM in Wantmecourt.	
	29		Captain the Marquis of Northampton Royal Horse Guards assumed command of the squadron vice Captain Shipwith 17th Cavalry ordered to rejoin his regiment. C. Shipwith	

MAISON-PONTHIEU

POSTS

Outgoing		Incoming
7.30 AM	GHQ troops, 3 Cav Div Billets Supply Column, 3rd Field Squadron Amm Park O.C.ASC DADR DADOS Can. Cav. Bde	1.30 PM
8 AM	6, 7, 8 Cav Bdes.	10 AM
9 AM	4th Bde RHA, 7 L.A.C. Battery, 3 F.S. Detacht.	9.30 AM
1.30 PM	Reserve Corps	1 PM
4 PM	GHQ troops 3 Cav Div Billets Supply Col. 3 F.S. Amm Park O.C.ASC, DADR DADOS. Can. Cav. Bde.	10 PM
4 PM	6, 7, 8 Cav Bdes	6 PM
5 PM	4th Bde RHA, 7 L.A.C. Battery, 3 F.S. Detacht.	5.30 PM
6.30 PM	Reserve Corps	10 PM

C. Skipwith Capt.
Comdg Signals 3 Cav Div

16/5/16

Vol 17. Army Form C.2118
3rd Signal Sqdn

June to August 1916

WAR DIARY

INTELLIGENCE SUMMARY
(Erase heading not required.)

Instructions regarding War Diaries and Intelligence Summaries are contained in F.S. Regs., Part II. and the Staff Manual respectively. Title Pages will be prepared in manuscript.

Place	Date	Hour	Summary of Events and Information	Remarks and references to Appendices
FRUGES	1/6/16		Early riding school but broken leg discouraged this for some time. Visual Signallers every afternoon at 2 need a deal of practice. Horses not doing sufficient work.	
	12th		Divided mounted men into sections of 4 men each under N.C.O. and each containing a Pigeon man or Saddler or Shoeing Smith to hold visual signallers horses when at work. Each section responsible for its own men, horses and signalling equipment.	
	?		Went into loading of waggons and altered details. Made no changes in existing circuits, but few alterations in office procedure.	
	15th		Divisional Scheme – all Signal Personnel to be out on trial – Divisional Report Centre remained several hours at certain X-roads – A Visual Central Station was established & connected to report centre by a mile of D5 cable. Cable laid in 5 minutes by motor trailer, but visual work very slow. No sun. DR's had very bad roads. 7th Brigade lost for 2 hours. In spite of warning on previous day Signal Troops bad at notifying change of Report Centre. Obtained urgently some French Cavalry Pattern of Pigeon Baskets. Tried to get use of a left out the pigeons were of a domestic breed – Pigeon men will never be happy till we have	

1875 Wt. W593/826 1,000,000 4/15 J.B.C. & A. A.D.S.S./Forms/C.2118.

WAR DIARY or INTELLIGENCE SUMMARY

Army Form C. 2118

3rd Signal Sqdn

Place	Date	Hour	Summary of Events and Information	Remarks and references to Appendices
FRUGES	15/6/16 17/6/16		JUNE (Contd) a loft of our own, which is impossible here. Practice wireless with aeroplanes - would be invaluable to cavalry warfare. Weather bad all week except one day, when messages dropped and reports received by wireless from an aeroplane. Captain James R.F.C. joined with 7 other ranks and a motor tender -	
	22nd		Picked up all lines except HD to VCR.	
	24th	6pm	Marched to FONTAINE-sur-MAYE with Brigades and Divnl Troops. JOC and Staff remaining at FRUGES for night. Communication by telephone from TORTEFONTAINE via HESDIN.	
	25th	8pm	Marched to DOMART-en-PONTHIEU. Communication by horse and telephone superimposed with 2CO - 2AR and VA. B rigades at ST OUEN etc. Communication by DR. Left Donbee Aircraft Set & other business in store.	
	26th	6pm	Marched to LA NEUVILLE - Communication with Reserve Army by horse and telephone superimposed - laid DS line to BONNAY where all Division was bivouacked in a marsh. Had great trouble with horses who appeared not to be fit - evacuated and received no reinforcements - also 4 horses 2 drivers and gs hubert wagon attached to cavalry	

WAR DIARY
or
INTELLIGENCE SUMMARY. 3rd Signal Sqdn

Army Form C. 2118.

Place	Date	Hour	Summary of Events and Information	Remarks and references to Appendices
LA NEUVILLE	27/6/16		aeroplane patrol — several zero days on each of which pigeons were borrowed from LAVIEVILLE loft, jt routes of advance were reconnoitred	
			McTavney Capt. 3rd Signal Sqdn	

Army Form C. 2118

WAR DIARY
INTELLIGENCE SUMMARY
(Erase heading not required.)

3rd Signal Sqdn

Place	Date	Hour	Summary of Events and Information	Remarks and references to Appendices
July	July 4th		marched to Hallencourt where established communication by horse & telephone with Abbeville and with 3 Brigades by Vibrator -	
	6th		line built to Cuirl and Supply Column at AIRAINES.	
	8th		marched to DAOURS. Hence telephonic communication with Brigades at VAUX, BONNAY and CORBIE through 13th Corps Exchange at CORBIE. Did a deal of helio work - 8 men went sick with boils -	Nothampton Coyn

WAR DIARY
INTELLIGENCE SUMMARY — 3rd Signal Squadron

Army Form C. 2118

Place	Date	Hour	Summary of Events and Information	Remarks and references to Appendices
August	1st	—	marched to LE QUESNOY whence 7th Brigade had communication with 23rd Div'n and Reserve Army.	
	2nd		marched to YVRENCH whence put through various lines to Brigades in neighbourhood of ST-RIQUIER.	
	4th		marched to LIGESCOURT	
	5th		marched to FRUGES area. But 8th Bde. went to ERIN.	

WAR DIARY or INTELLIGENCE SUMMARY

Army Form C. 2118

3 Cav Signal Sqn

Place	Date	Hour	Summary of Events and Information	Remarks and references to Appendices
FRUGES	5 August 6th and 7th		Laid temporary cable from TRAMECOURT to ERIN. Laid 40 lb bronze line to HUCQUELIER and 9.lb.iron line to ROYON. Latter line only as temporary - 23 men not working. Cleared all old wiring out of office and simplified wiring. Issued trench telephones galore. But Staff clamoured for C.2.'s.	
	10th		Fairly high completed Wireless Receiving Set (no closed circuit) and daily English French German & Austrian communiqués taken. 6th Bde "moved" to Embry where Td on to 7th line at Henoville.	
	12th		ROYON to TORCY line picket up. Alternate days riding school & visual signalling throughout the month which gives the horses alternate days grazing. Driving is never sufficiently enforced by NCO's. Deliver lecture to them on this. Driving drill by Sergt Major for ten days to all except m/cyclists. Lectured on Telephony.	

Northampton Capt.

WAR DIARY
or
~~INTELLIGENCE SUMMARY~~

(Erase heading not required.)

Army Form C. 2118

Vol 2 3rd Signal Sqdn

Instructions regarding War Diaries and Intelligence Summaries are contained in F.S. Regs., Part II. and the Staff Manual respectively. Title Pages will be prepared in manuscript.

Place	Date	Hour	Summary of Events and Information	Remarks and references to Appendices
FRUGES	SEPTEMBER 10th		Left FRUGES for DOMPIERRE — Divnl HQrs remaining at TRAMECOURT	
	11th		Marched to MAISON PONTHIEU — used telegraph office at YVRENCH	
	12th		Marched to BELLOY-S/SOMME where telephonic communication with 10th Corps and all Bdes.	
	14th		Marched to DAOURS	
	22nd		Marched to LE QUESNOY whence telegraph + telephone to 10th Corps	
	23rd		Marched to FROHEN-LE-GRAND whence telegraph + telephone to DOULENS.	
	24th		Marched to CAPELLE with Divnl HQrs at FOND de MOURIEZ, whence telegraph + telephone to HESDIN. Brigades moved several times — and settled with 6th at VERTON, 8th at BRIMEUX, each connected by telegraph to g HQ (8th also on g HQ exchange); and 7th at FRESSIN whence joined by cable to HESDIN — FRUGES line and on HD exchange —	

Northampton Capt.
3rd Signal Sqdn

Army Form C. 2118

WAR DIARY
or
INTELLIGENCE SUMMARY • 3rd SIGNAL SQDN
(Erase heading not required.)

Vol 21

Place	Date	Hour	Summary of Events and Information	Remarks and references to Appendices
			OCTOBER -16	
MOURIEZ	18/10/16		Divnal HQrs moved to WAILLY whence Vibrator line to VERTON and those direct to PH superimposed on Telephone Pair to 7HQ. Also single wire to 2CO at REGNIERE ECLUSE with 7HQ intermediate. Local pairs to BOIS JEAN, LAHOUSSOIE, General Staff, Q Staff, A SC, Stables. And lines to Divisional Schools at MERLIMONT PLAGE and Chateau NE of WAILLY. Tried superimposing on more line to former but too much noise on line for speaking. Built Vibrator line towards FRESSIN but was ordered to pick it up by ADAS.	Northampton Capt

WAR DIARY
or
~~INTELLIGENCE SUMMARY~~

(Erase heading not required.)

Army Form C. 2118

November 1916

Vol 22

Place	Date	Hour	Summary of Events and Information	Remarks and references to Appendices
Wailly			9 H.Q. Signals built pair of lines to each Brigade. The S.C. Sets without relays would not give satisfaction however over a circuit 7 miles long. Lines built to 3rd Field Squadron + C Battery Class of NCO's Nov 14th to Dec 2nd Classes of officers Nov 20th to Dec 2nd Dec 5th to 10th	

Northampton
Capt
3rd Signal Sqdn.

WAR DIARY

or

INTELLIGENCE SUMMARY

(Erase heading not required.)

Army Form C. 2118

3rd Signal Squadron

WM 23

Place	Date	Hour	Summary of Events and Information	Remarks and references to Appendices
	DECEMBER			
	19th		Moved to TREPIED. All horses + most mounted men left at WAILLY until stables could be built. Office left at WAILLY with local subexchange + morse intermediate between VC and PF at VERTON. Paris direct to 2Co and to G.H.Q.	
	22nd		6th Bde to MARESQUEL - morse to J MQ. 8th Bde to VERTON - telephone to WAILLY exchange - morse through to TREPIED.	
	28th		Cavalry Corps take on subexchange at WAILLY - 1 DR left there.	
	31st		GOC presented Military medal to L/Cpl H. Gooch and Sapper Southworth.	

Montcompt Cew

WAR DIARY
or
~~INTELLIGENCE SUMMARY~~

Army Form C. 2118

Vol 24

3rd SIGNAL SQDN

JANUARY 1917

Place	Date	Hour	Summary of Events and Information	Remarks and references to Appendices
15th			Course of 21 new hands all in the Divn — duration 3 weeks 6 Officers	
27th			Lt. J. H. Fairclough ordered to report to 8th Corps Signals left on 3/2/17.	

Northampton. Capt.
3rd Signal Sqdn.

Army Form C. 2118

WAR DIARY
~~INTELLIGENCE SUMMARY~~
(Erase heading not required.)

Vol 25

Instructions regarding War Diaries and Intelligence Summaries are contained in F.S. Regs., Part II. and the Staff Manual respectively. Title Pages will be prepared in manuscript.

Place	Date	Hour	Summary of Events and Information 3rd SIGNAL SQUDN FEBRUARY 1917	Remarks and references to Appendices
	18th		Cpl CLEMENTS presented with Military Medal.	
	26th		Course for week for Regimental Sergt. Instructors.	
	28th		1 Officer, 8 men and 11 horses attached for Extrct work with RFC.	

Northampers Capt.

Army Form C. 2118

WAR DIARY
or
INTELLIGENCE SUMMARY
(Erase heading not required.)

Vol 26

3rd Signal Sqdn

Instructions regarding War Diaries and Intelligence Summaries are contained in F. S. Regs., Part II. and the Staff Manual respectively. Title Pages will be prepared in manuscript.

Place	Date	Hour	Summary of Events and Information	Remarks and references to Appendices
			MARCH 1917	
			Final Stages of Training :-	
			Wolsampton	Capn.

WAR DIARY
INTELLIGENCE SUMMARY
(Erase heading not required.)

Army Form C. 2118

Vol 27

3rd Signal Sqdn

Instructions regarding War Diaries and Intelligence Summaries are contained in F. S. Regs., Part II. and the Staff Manual respectively. Title Pages will be prepared in manuscript.

Place	Date	Hour	Summary of Events and Information	Remarks and references to Appendices
Tropied	1st 5th 7th 8th 9th		Pack Wireless Section joined from Cavalry Corps. Marched to MARESQUEL connected 2co via JHQ. MONCHEL. 2co via CAR. GOUY-EN-ARTOIS.	
	9th	10am	position of readiness just west of ARRAS.	
		2pm	Advanced to TILLOY les MOFFLAINES. Enemy had not retired as far as anticipated. Divl HQrs returned to ARRAS for the night moved forward to TILLOY. Reconnaissances sent forward round MONCHY but unable to do so.	
	10th		Divisional report centre remained on ridge near ESTAMINET CORNER north of ARRAS-CAMBRAI road till 9 pm 11th. Communication by visual all day, except for occasional Snow-Showers, to the Brigade HQrs on ORANGE HILL also by Mounted Orderly. The latter took average of 35 mins. No communication with MONCHY except from Bdes by Mtd Orderly. Cavalry Corps cable arrived about 11 am 10th. marched back to GOUY. WAVANS. LIGESCOURT where 7th Bde direct + 8th Brigade via 2co. direct. North army Corps ASC at Rephauville	communication with 6th Bde through PG.
	12th 16th 19th			

1875 Wt. W593/826 1,000,000 4/15 J.B.C. & A. A.D.S.S./Forms/C. 2118.

WAR DIARY
INTELLIGENCE SUMMARY

Signals 3rd Divisional Squadron

Army Form C. 2118.

Month: May 1917

Place	Date	Hour	Summary of Events and Information	Remarks and references to Appendices
LIGESCOURT	1st		Usual squadron parades.	
	2nd			
	3rd			
	4th			
	5th			
	6th			
	7th			
	8th		C.O.C. inspected the squadron.	
	9th		Usual squadron parades.	
	10th			
	11th			
	12th			
	13th		Capt. Lisle H. Lancers assumed command of the Squadron vice Capt. L.F. Nervin Bridington who returned to his regiment. The Royal Horse Guards to take up regimental duties. Lt Mackintyre 20th Hussars joined the squadron vice 2/Lt Bailey returned to Cavalry Corps Signals	
BEAUVOIR WAVANS	13th		Squadron marched to BEAUVOIR WAVANS. Communications established to Signals and Cavalry Corps.	
TALMAS	14th		Marched to TALMAS. Established communication to 3rd Army H.Q.s through time exchange we were in touch with G.H.Q.	
QUERRIEU	15th		Squadron marched to QUERRIEU. Lifted alongside 4th Army Signal Office. Took over existing communications to Rail Corps ab G Army & 2 Signals.	
	16th		2 B O.R. left Squadron to form 2nd Cav Composite Signal Sq.	

WAR DIARY or INTELLIGENCE SUMMARY

Army Form C. 2118.

May 1914 Signals 2nd Divisional Squadron

Place	Date	Hour	Summary of Events and Information	Remarks and references to Appendices
LAMOTTE	14/5		Moved to LAMOTTE-EN-SANTERRE. Communications established to Cavalry Depot. Lt. Houghton & 20 OR handed over to Cav Corps Signals. H pack wireless detachment left for duty with Cav Corps Signals	
	18th		Usual squadron parades	
	19th		Signaling practice. Communications established to Cav Corps through PERONNE civil exchange.	
	20th		Capt. Horby-Moore G.D.Gds assumed command of the squadron vice Capt Dingle 2nd Lancers returned to Cav Corps Signals. Lt Williams (R.A.) rejoined the squadron. 2 OR from Cav Corps Signals & 4 OR reinforcements joined the squadron	
PAMICOURT	21st		9 OR from 1st K.L.R.M.B. joined the squadron	
	22nd		3 OR reinforcements " "	
	23rd		Usual squadron parades. Orders received to move to a forward area at sh 34 F	
	24		3 Officers and 59 OR marched to E.29.a.9.6 (63C) the remainder of the squadron being left in PAMICOURT to maintain a small signal office signed there & to look after the horses	

WAR DIARY
INTELLIGENCE SUMMARY

Army Form C. 2118.

May 1917.

Signals
a Divisional Squadron

Place	Date	Hour	Summary of Events and Information	Remarks and references to Appendices
ERZA 90 VILLERS FAUCON	24	8.45am	Communication established to forward Brigades, Corps and Brigades in rear.	
	25		Line laid to G.T. Office and tactics busy strengthening lines erected. Div. Corps Signals 90 megaphones referred.	
	26		Line laid to advanced field squadron. Forward Brigade office reconstructed. 50 megaphones and security (B.) issued.	
	27		Most of the cable laid but retrieved. Air line (B. Service) turnout.	
	28 to 30		The system of communication made permanent & semi-permanent.	
	31		Lt Collins Strathcona Horse joined the squadron. A squadron of Private attached.	

Haley Lieut.
Z. / Sig. Sq.

Signals 3rd Divisional Squadron. WAR DIARY

3 June 1917. Vol 29

Army Form C. 2118.

INTELLIGENCE SUMMARY.
(Erase heading not required)

Instructions regarding War Diaries and Intelligence Summaries are contained in F.S. Regs., Part II. and the Staff Manual respectively. Title pages will be prepared in manuscript.

Place	Date	Hour	Summary of Events and Information	Remarks and references to Appendices
VILLERS FAUCON. E.23.a.9.6.	1st to 27th		Communications the same as from the 24th May with the exception that an alternative route was established between this office and our forward brigade at F.1.D.8.8. Lines in forward brigade strengthened & new cables built. From 18th to 24th the weather was very varying. Heavy thunderstorms + violent winds causing a considerable amount of trouble to the lines.	Reference sheet 62. 1/40,000
	28th		Our forward brigade office at the HQ F.1.D.8.8 taken over by 2nd Cav Div BEtts Brigade.	
	29th to 30th		6th, 7th & 8th Cav Bdes working through Cavalry Corps to our office. Locations J.24.D.4.6 J.22.D.5.0. J.32.C.5.6 respectively.	
	30th		Local circuits working from this office. All other circuits through 2nd Cav Div except 1 Cav Corps which is direct.	

F. Farley Moore Capt
O.C.
3rd Signal Squadron.

Circuit Diagram

3rd Cavalry Division June 1917.

References
— Air-line
---- Cable
∿∿ Wireless

Villers Faucon — 3rd Cav Div HQ Qrs.
- Sqdn Office → Staff Capt.
- O.C Fd Sqdn → Y.C.E
- Sig. Mess
- A.D.M.S
- D.D.M.S
- G.S
- Q

Z.C.O.
- V.C.
- P.O. Details
- Transport
- P.F.
- P.H.
- Peronne
- Q.O.
- V.B
- QF Help
- HT
- Rt Support Bn

Epehy — H.K.
- (Amplifier)
- Bde Office
- Lt. Support Bn
- Support Sqdn
- Outpost
- Birdcage
- Outpost x20 d 84
- Power Buzzer
- N.23 d 88 Hind

Circuit references: 55-56, 59-60, 53-54, 51-52

WAR DIARY
or
INTELLIGENCE SUMMARY.

Army Form C. 2118.

Signals   3rd Divisional Sgn. (I.)

July 1916   Vol 30

Place	Date	Hour	Summary of Events and Information	Remarks and references to Appendices
VILLERS FAUCON	1st		Marched to FLAMICOURT opened communications at 11 a.m. to 6th & 7th & 8th Brigades via 2 CO.	
FLAMICOURT	2nd		The 8th Bde. Sdn. moved to SUZANNE comm. established through PERONNE – MARICOURT exchange, morse & telephone. 8th Bde.	
	3rd		6th & 7th Bdes moved to SUZANNE area comm. morse & telephone. Bde. to HEILLY comm. telephone.	
	4th		6th Bde. Bde HEILLY 7th S. of MARICOURT 8th ORVILLE Divisional HQ TREUX. Communication with Div. to Bdes 1.15 pm. Other comm. morse & telephone at 12 noon.	
TREUX	5th		6th Bde. ORVILLE 7th HEILLY 8th ETREE WAMIN Div HQ DOULLENS comm. opened 12 noon morse & telephone.	
DOULLENS	6th		6th Bde. REBRUVIETTE comm. by telephone via PREVENT ST POL exchanges 7th Bde. ORVILLE comm. via DOULLENS ST POL 8th Bde. DIEVAL comm. by D.R. only. DIV HQ SAINS comm. telephone via ST POL telegraph circuits in ST POL.	
SAINS	7th		6th Bde. AUCHEL comm. telephone via 1st Army. 7th Bde. REBRUVIETTE comm. telephone via PREVENT ST POL 8th Bde. DIEVAL comm. telephone via 4 & 6 DIV DIV HQ PERNES In comm. with 1st, 2nd & 3rd ARMIES & all subordinate units	

WAR DIARY or INTELLIGENCE SUMMARY

Army Form C. 2118.

Signals — 3rd Divisional Squadron

July 1914.

Instructions regarding War Diaries and Intelligence Summaries are contained in F.S. Regs., Part II. and the Staff Manual respectively. Title pages will be prepared in manuscript.

(Erase heading not required.)

Place	Date	Hour	Summary of Events and Information	Remarks and references to Appendices
PERNES	8th		6th Cav Bde AUCHEL ⎫ In communication wire & telephone to DIV HQ 7th Cav Bde BERNES ⎬ VIA 1st ARMY LILLERS. 8th Cav Bde DIEVAL ⎭	
	9th to 15th		No change of stations. Some communication as on the 8th.	
	16th		DIV HQ marched to BUSNES wire established to 3 Brigades & Cav Corps & 1st Army 6th Cav Bde LES LAURIER wire VIA MERVILLE wire telephone direct 7th Cav Bde AUCHEL wire telephone.	
BUSNES	17th		7th Cav Bde GUARDBECQUE wire. VIA ST YENANT wire. telephone direct 8th Cav Bde THIENNES wire wire VIA 2CO telephone direct.	
	18th to 31st		No change of stations. Visual signalling schemes carried out when weather permitted. Usual squadron parades.	

F. Harley Moore Capt.
D.O.
3rd Signal Sqdn R.E.

August 1914.

Army Form C. 2118.

WAR DIARY
or
INTELLIGENCE SUMMARY.

Signals
5th Divisional Squadron.

No 31

(Erase heading not required.)

Instructions regarding War Diaries and Intelligence Summaries are contained in F.S. Regs., Part II. and the Staff Manual respectively. Title pages will be prepared in manuscript.

Place	Date	Hour	Summary of Events and Information	Remarks and references to Appendices
BUSNES	1st	9.30 9.45 10.45 12.30 10—	Usual squadron parades & visual signalling schemes when the weather permitted. Signalling schemes in conjunction with aeroplanes 8th Don. Squ. moved from THIENNES to HAM EN ARTOIS connected up by wire & telephone via Cavalry Divl.	
	12.15 31st		No further movement of Brigade. Visual schemes carried out when possible.	

H Harby Sml Capt.
D.O.
3rd Div Sqdn.

September 1917

Army Form C. 2118.

WAR DIARY
or
INTELLIGENCE SUMMARY

Signals 3rd Divisional Squadron

Vol 32

Place	Date	Hour	Summary of Events and Information	Remarks and references to Appendices
BUSNES	1st to 30		Divnal. Squadron Parades. Visual Signalling Schemes with Aeroplanes & Kite Balloons carried out when possible	

F. Harley Moor
O.D.
3rd Sig Sqdn.

WAR DIARY

October 1917

Signals — 3rd Divisional Squadron
Sheet No 1

Army Form C. 2118.

INTELLIGENCE SUMMARY

Place	Date	Hour	Summary of Events and Information	Remarks and references to Appendices
BUSNES	1st to 9th		Usual squadron routine. Visual Schemes & mounted D.R. exercises carried out.	
	10th		7th CAV BDE from PERNES to MERVILLE communication via 1st ARMY.	
	11th		8th CAV BDE from HAM-EN-ARTOIS to RUE-DE-GUARDBEQUE comm. via ST VENANT exchange.	
	12th to 13th		Usual squadron parade. Schemes with Kite Balloon.	
	16th		DIV HQ from BUSNES to PERNES comm. on direct trunk to CORPS morse & telephone.	
	17th		8th CAV BDE to PRESSY LES PERNES comm. telephone only.	
PERNES	18th		6th CAV BDE to TANGRY comm. morse & telephone comm. through PREVENT.	
	19th		8th CAV BDE to REBREUVE telephone comm. through PREVENT. 8th CAV BDE hung intermediate.	
	20th		7th CAV BDE to TANGRY telephone comm. via ST POL exchange.	
	21st		8th CAV BDE to VIGNACOURT comm. by DR service. 6th CAV BDE to REBREUVE telephone comm. via PREVENT	
	22nd		DIV HQ to HOUVIN HOUVIGNEUS comm. telephone & supermorse moves to CORPS via ST POL.	
	23rd		DIV HQ to DOMART-EN-PONTHIEU telephone & move to CORPS at BEAUGESNE. 8th CAV BDE to GORENFLOS comm. by DR service. 7th CAV BDE to REBREUVE comm. telephone via PREVENT. 8th CAV BDE through to DIV telephone & supermorse direct front. All local lines laid.	
	24th		7th CAV BDE to RIBECOURT comm. telephone & move via CORPS. Underground circuit. 6th CAV BDE to LONGUET comm. by DR service	

L. Stanley Moore Capt.
Cmd. 3rd SIGNAL SQUADRON, R.E.

Army Form C. 2118.

WAR DIARY
of
Signals
INTELLIGENCE SUMMARY. 3rd Divisional Squadron.

October 1917

App No 1

Instructions regarding War Diaries and Intelligence Summaries are contained in F. S. Regs., Part II. and the Staff Manual respectively. Title pages will be prepared in manuscript.

(Erase heading not required.)

Place	Date	Hour	Summary of Events and Information	Remarks and references to Appendices
DOMART	25th		Arrangements being made to get PC on to a direct pair.	
	26th		Reconnoitring links in area with a view to putting regiments onto their Brigades.	
	27th		Establishing communication with 6th CAV BDE on a direct pair.	
	28th		6th CAV BDE in comm with DIV means & telephone.	
	29th		No change.	
	30th		LEIC YEO direct wire to DIV EXC.	
	31st		No change.	

H Stanley Smyth ..... Capt.
O.md. 3rd SIGNAL SQUADRON, R.E.

WAR DIARY or INTELLIGENCE SUMMARY

Army Form C. 2118.

Signals 3rd Divisional Squadron

Vol 34

November 1914.

Place	Date	Hour	Summary of Events and Information	Remarks and references to Appendices
DONART	1st to 4th		Usual squadron parades & the straightening up of lines in this new area.	
	5th		A G.I pair on horse polo built to Y.H. CAV BDE avail from DUMART to RIBEAUCOURT.	
	6th		A G.I pair built to 14th BDE R.H.A. at LA HAIE FARM.	
	7th to 15th		Usual parades & scheme of instruction with visual schemes.	
	16th			
	17th		6th & 7th CAV BDES to CONTAY area a joint office established for the two.	
SUZANNE	18th		Div to SUZANNE a direct pair to 2CO & C.A.R.	
	19th		Through to forward office by I.B.C. at FINS. Lines to P.H. PF & PG	
	20th		No change	
	21st			
	22nd		DIV H.Q. to BEAUQUESNE. 6th CAV BDE to TALMAS. 7th CAV BDE to BEAUCOURT. 8th CAV BDE to BERTANGLES	
			Lines given by 3rd Army. Working in more improved.	
	23rd to 29th		No change	
	30th		DIV H.Q. to CORBIE communication to the CORPS the Brigades in rear.	
			Messages dealt with during month 3289. Exchange calls 4420. Labs & kits 368	

Halemore Capt.
O.C.
3rd Sig Sqdn

December 1914. WAR DIARY or INTELLIGENCE SUMMARY. 3rd Divisional Squadron Signals.
Army Form C. 2118.
Vol 35

Place	Date	Hour	Summary of Events and Information	Remarks and references to Appendices
CORBIE	1st		3rd Div Div Boie to BERNES. Telephone route Circulation 24th Div–VII CORPS, ZRC, ZCO.	Sh 57 62C.
	2nd		6 L Bar Boie details from TALMAS to MOUFLERS–PU–BOIS	
			8 L Bar Boie details from BERTANGLES to BELLOY SUR SOMME	
	3rd		3rd Bar Boie on telephone via AMIENS exchange	
	4th		No change.	
	5th			
	6th			
	7th		3rd Bar Div Bde took over from 14 Inf Bde of the 24th Div – HQ 2 R 8 b 53	
	8th			
	9th			
	20th		No change.	
	21st		Div Div HQ to BOUYENCOURT moved to CAV CORPS 12 noon	
	22nd		G.O.C. 10th Divn (3rd CAV DIV) resumed command 10 a.m. 8" "D" Betty Anti Aircraft 10 a.m.	
			(1.) Through on Lines 2CO 10 a.m. Ours all local circuits	
			Superpaired 2CO 2 p.m.	
			(2.) To VII Corps on phone 10 a.m.	
			(3.) To 2d Div " 10 a.m.	
			" Superspeed 8 p.m.	
			(4.) " 2nd Div Div on phone 11 a.m.	
			" " " Superspeed 6 p.m.	
			(5.) " 3rd " " Phone 11 a.m.	
			" " " Superspeed 3.20 p.m.	
			(6.) French Cable Group 11 a.m.	
			(7.) HQ + H Bde 2 Co 10 a.m.	

Place	Date	Hour	Summary of Events and Information	Remarks and references to Appendices
BOUVINCOURT	23rd		Through to FRENCH MISSION & ADMS on plans at GOUVINCOURT. Cut off 2nd Bty Anti aircraft & French Arty Group.	
	24th		Through to FRENCH Sn. Dn. on night 11am supernumary moves 2 p.m.	
	25th		Xmas Day. No change.	
	26th		Had our usual Reps 9X re why of PO at Cy.d.6.3. The whole notes place tomorrow. Applied to DO w/t CAVCORPS for movement of DLP (Tunnels) PO & A) to centre sector also PO & A to relieve that at Cy b & 2. One PO & A for cav. French fraction suggested by Gen Campbell CRE Div. Div requested to build suitable dugouts.	
	27th		The French cut at RIIC8.8. cannot be moved until CRE builds recommenced. All lines O.K.	
	28th		Informed entire sector in connection with similar groups. One happy going accommodation furnished for PO & A & Headquarters the cav. The CRE Div Divn cannot promise Tunnelling completed before arrival.	
	29th		Lines for Artillery group made over to Capt. Bullen. Reps 40 Arty Div. HQ at ENVINCOURT. The French Quitting will be in course on a French civil paid from Bedret, the part allotted by French Div. Morning late all clear. SSO at TINCOURT through on TINCOURT exchange	

Army Form C. 2118.

WAR DIARY
or
INTELLIGENCE SUMMARY.
(Erase heading not required.)

Instructions regarding War Diaries and Intelligence Summaries are contained in F. S. Regs., Part II. and the Staff Manual respectively. Title pages will be prepared in manuscript.

Place	Date	Hour	Summary of Events and Information	Remarks and references to Appendices
BOUINCOURT	30		Through to French Arty via R.H.A. (BOUINCOURT who under Div Cav Regt.) carried up an exchange. Through to R & L Group Arty via RHA HQ. "C" CAYCORPS HEAVIES 10 a.m. "I" 24.Div (alternative line made over to RHA HQ. All numbered as detached by CAY CORPS served out. Route & circuit diagrams being finished.	L. Stanley Groves Capt. O.D. Div Divn Signals

WAR DIARY or INTELLIGENCE SUMMARY

Signals. 3rd Divisional Signal Squadron

Army Form C. 2118.

Vol 36

January 1918

Place	Date	Hour	Summary of Events and Information	Remarks and references to Appendices
BOUVINCOURT	1st & 2nd		No change	
	3rd		Air line route built from Sigs DO Dump to HQ RHA in same village all cable picked up. RHA Wagon lines at CAULAINCOURT put through on lines. MDS at POEUILLY put through on line to MDS at BOUVINCOURT. Throughout each night patrols up cable where possible twenty cable faults during the night.	
	3rd to 21st			
	22nd		Remainder of Div Signs moved to yr CAVDIV at 10 am. Handed over all tageuf route circuit & rate diagrams to CAPT GODRINGTON. Opened up at DOMART-EN-PONTHIEU 10 a.p.m. Communication with PF PG and PH mares & telephone also to CAV CORPS via DERUQUESNE & 5th ARMY.	
	23rd to 29th		No change	
MONCHY LE BREUC	30th		Open HQ established where the Div Sigs Left. Nought. to CORPS. PH & PF. YC being intermediate. All local wind.	
	31st		Communication with PG at MAROEUIL CAVE by DR's only. Hqrs move to TREPCON tomorrow	

L Darby Moore Capt.
O.C. 3rd Div Sig Sqn

WAR DIARY
or
INTELLIGENCE SUMMARY. 3rd Divisional Squadron.

Army Form C. 2118.

February 1918 Signals

Vol 37

Place	Date	Hour	Summary of Events and Information	Remarks and references to Appendices
MONCHY LE PREUX	1st		O.R. to TREFCON superimposed under.	
	2nd / 18th		No change.	
	19th			
	20th		Line built DR to 14 Div. B.H.Q.	
	21st		No change	
	22nd			
	23rd			
	24th		Route built from MERROCOURT to DENISE.	
	25th			
	26th		No change	
	27th			
	28th			

Stanley Simone Capt
O.C. 3rd Div Sqdn

Army Form C. 2118.

WAR DIARY
or
INTELLIGENCE SUMMARY.
(Erase heading not required)

France 1918   3rd Aerial Sqn. R.E.

Place	Date	Hour	Summary of Events and Information	Remarks and references to Appendices
MONCHY LA GACHE	9th/10th		Court of enquiry parade and Grand Chants	
	11th		Lieut R.S. Stancliffe 2nd Life Gds assumed command vice Capt F. Farley. Moore to Cav Corps Signals	
	12th		No change.	
ATHIES	13th		Communications. Superimposed to 2CO, TCO, PF (Devise), PG (M Breancourt) PH (St Emilie) PCA (Ennemain)	
	14th		PH Leave the Divn. PA put on and Superimposed. Lt H.K. Chase 7th S.Gs appointed to duty.	
	15th/16th		No change.	
	17th		PG to ST CHRIST - PA to MEREAUCOURT.	
BEAUMONT SUR BEINE	18th to 20th to 21st		No change.	
VARESNES	22nd		VCR opened 8pm Beaumont-sur-Beine Superimposed to CCO. VC opened 12 Noon Varesnes.	
	23rd		VCR opened Beaumont. Phone to 108 Inf Bde and II Corps.	
	24th		VCR opened Muiracourt no telephone communication.	

WAR DIARY
or
INTELLIGENCE SUMMARY.
(Erase heading not required.)

Army Form C. 2118.

3rd Signal Sqdn.

March 1918

Place	Date	Hour	Summary of Events and Information	Remarks and references to Appendices
MOYENCOURT	24.		Close down 3.30 a.m. Marched to E. end of LAGNY arriving 6.30 a.m.	
LAGNY	25		Forward Relay Post opened at 2pm at CARTIGNY. Composed of four mounted Despatch Riders to take reports from motor cyclists forward to CAVALRY DETACHMENT HQrs in neighbourhood of CHEVILLY. [VC opened at OLLENCOURT]	
DIVES	26		Report Centre moved to DIVES 3.30 a.m. All communications found Carried by mounted Despatch Riders. [VC opened CROISY AU BAC]	
THIRESCOURT			Report Centre moved to THIRESCOURT 4.30 p.m. Report Centre moved to ELINCOURT 6.30 p.m.	
CHOISY AU BAC	27		Advanced HQrs marched to CROISY AU BAC. Four mounted D.R's and four motor cyclists Remained with Col REYNOLDS DETACHMENT.	
	28		No change	
LE MESNIL SAINS	29		Report Centre opened at LE MESNIL 2pm.	
EN AMIENOIS	30		VCR opened SAINS-EN-AMIENOIS 10 a.m. Phone to XIX Corps. VC opened WAILLY.	
	31.		Lt A.B. JOHNS 7th D.G. reported vice Capt G.S. COLLINS.	

3rd Signal Sqdn

Circuit Diagram of Communications.

V.C. — March 21st 1918.

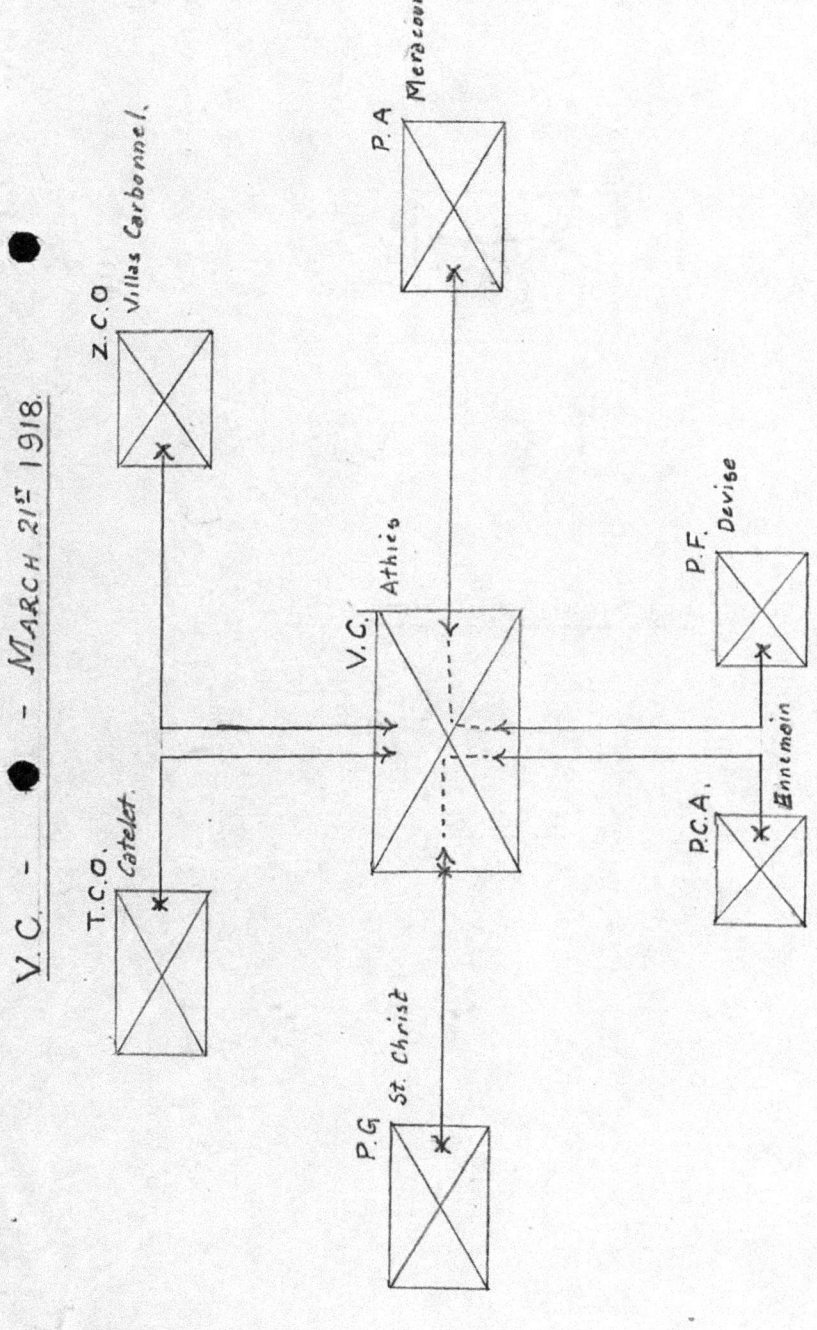

3rd Cav.Div.

WAR DIARY

3rd SIGNAL SQUADRON, R.E.

A P R I L

1 9 1 8

Attached:

Appendices A, B, C, D & E.

INTELLIGENCE SUMMARY.

(Erase heading not required.)

2nd Signal Sqn. RQ.

April 1918.

Place	Date	Hour	Summary of Events and Information	Remarks and references to Appendices
CHÂTEAU GRANDT BOVES	1st		Report Cable opened 7am. Telephone Trunks to PROVES EXCH. Telephone from 6th and 7th Cav Bde. 3rd Cav Div near on Telephone at PONT DE METZ. 6th and 7th Bde. moved late to Lt Pt BLANGY. CABARET. Telephone pair started by Corps. Arrived LONGEAU 7EST.	
BLANGY-TROUVILLE	2nd	4pm 5pm 6pm 9.45pm	Report Cable opened 2pm TRONVILLE CHATEAU. Telephone Communication with 19th Corps. Thus by 6th and 7th Cav Bdes to Lt Pt BLANGY CABARET. Thus to Cav Cl Pm at BOVES Clan. Cable with 200 on H/T. Superimposed & 19th Corps.	
	3rd	Office 5pm	Conoid. Squadron spent the day overhauling network. Equipment, rather Cable etc. 6th Cav Bde Bivouac'd to Pt Col Bon.	
FOUILLOY	4th	10am 3pm 7pm	RE went to FOUILLOY. With Bde H.Q.R. Bde office opened wiry. Connected to 6th Bde from FOUILLOY Office. Communication keen. Coil to 14/2 Inf Bde. 15th Aus Bde. Lt Cav Bde. another on the Thurl blue Verd, obtained by Lts Reid once former of Bne. In Wed SRS from Ca Corps to arct.	
BLANGY-TROUVILLE	5th	8pm 9pm	BLANGY OFFICE. Communication found to FOUILLOY and 19th Corps on a 2nd pair. Communication found the intermediate RE by new pair. Airline & Wagon line formed from MOLIENS. Sit Aus Inf Bne Sig'd Cty Cent on Communication.	See Appendix 'A'
RIVERY	6th		Report SRE Cable moved to RIVERY office. Liaison arm from VB. Con. air telegram and Airline of am. Telephone Commun other thro' Amiens MD. 6th Cav Bde, 3 Camon. 7th Cav Bde LA MOTTE BRETIERE.	See Appendix 'B'
	7th/9th		Squadron duties and parties Reports at loops. No event to communicate.	

APRIL 1918   3rd Sqnd Squadron RAF.

(Erase heading not required.)

Place	Date	Hour	Summary of Events and Information	Remarks and references to Appendices
RIVERY.	10th		A.M. Car Capt. Arrived & Querrieu-Chateau. V.C. took over this Office. Superimposed to 2CO and DAP.	SEE APPENDIX C
AUXI LE CHATEAU.	11th		Official Dinner. 2CO told all Officers of his Exchange, also 7th Cavalle Occurred. 2nd Car Car Run DRAWING. 6 Mile Run. Burial av Corps. VC took DR's office only.	
ST POL PERNES.	12th	3pm	R.C. & ST POL Signal Office	
		6.30pm	RC opened in PERNES. Superimposed to 2BC FOURRAGE.	
	13th		6th Ca Rue FERFAY. Superimposed.	See APPENDIX D
			7th Ca Bde. FLORINGHEM. Phone to PERNES EXCHANGE.	
			Canadian CONTEVILLE D.R. only	
	14th		4th Bde RHQ moved to PERNES.	
	15th		7th Ca Rue & MOLINGHEM BROOK. Phone thru 4th Cops and LPS.	
	16th		7th Cav Bde to PERNES. Telephone.	See APPENDIX E
			Ca A Rue to BOYAVAL. Superimposed to VA.	
	17th		No change.	
	18th		No change.	
	19th		No change.	
	20th		Aeroplane Phone with No 6 Sqn R.A.F. Receiving messages from Aeroplane sent in Clear.	
	21st/23rd		No Change.	
	24th		W/T Rels. to FONTAINE LES HERMANS.	
	25th		No Change.	

INTELLIGENCE SUMMARY.

3rd Scout Squadron N.Z.

(Erase heading not required)

APRIL 1918

Place	Date	Hour	Summary of Events and Information	Remarks and references to Appendices
FRANCE	26	1.10 pm	B⁰ Orders on the telephone	
	27		7th Order for BOYAVAL 12 noon, took over from CANADIAN Rd. Can Base for VERCHIN 12 noon	
	28	2 pm	Troops & Canadians on Prime kit VA and APR.	
		7.50pm	VA & principals to Canadian Rd.	
	29	12.40 pm	VA Cars Alexandria between VA and 2CP	
		3.20 pm	VA intermediate between PA and etc.	
	30	3.40 pm	Three direct to PF	
		7.15 pm	Superiors to PF.	

J Wardrift Capt
3rd Scout Squadron N.Z.
30/4/18

APPENDICES

A, B, C, D and E.

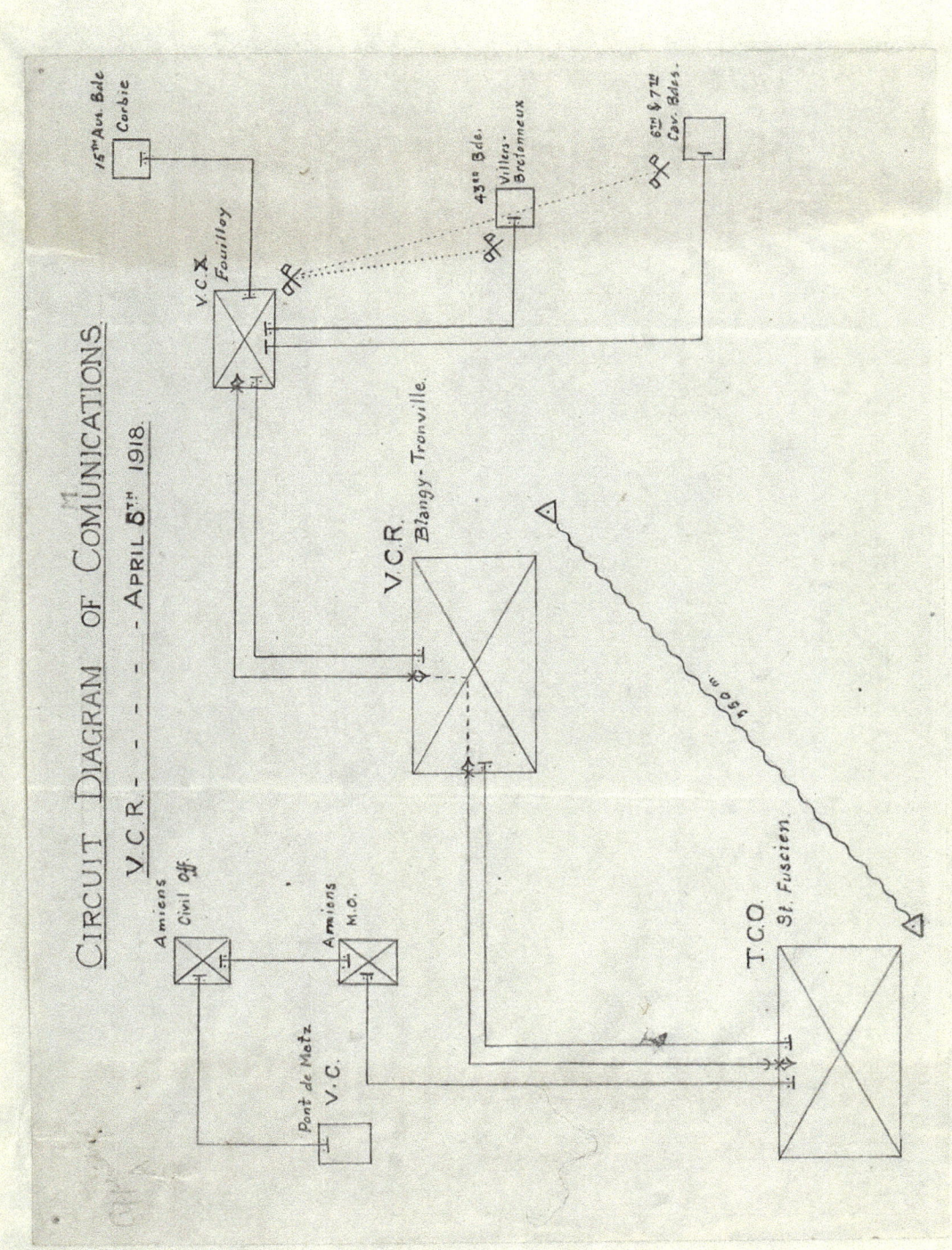

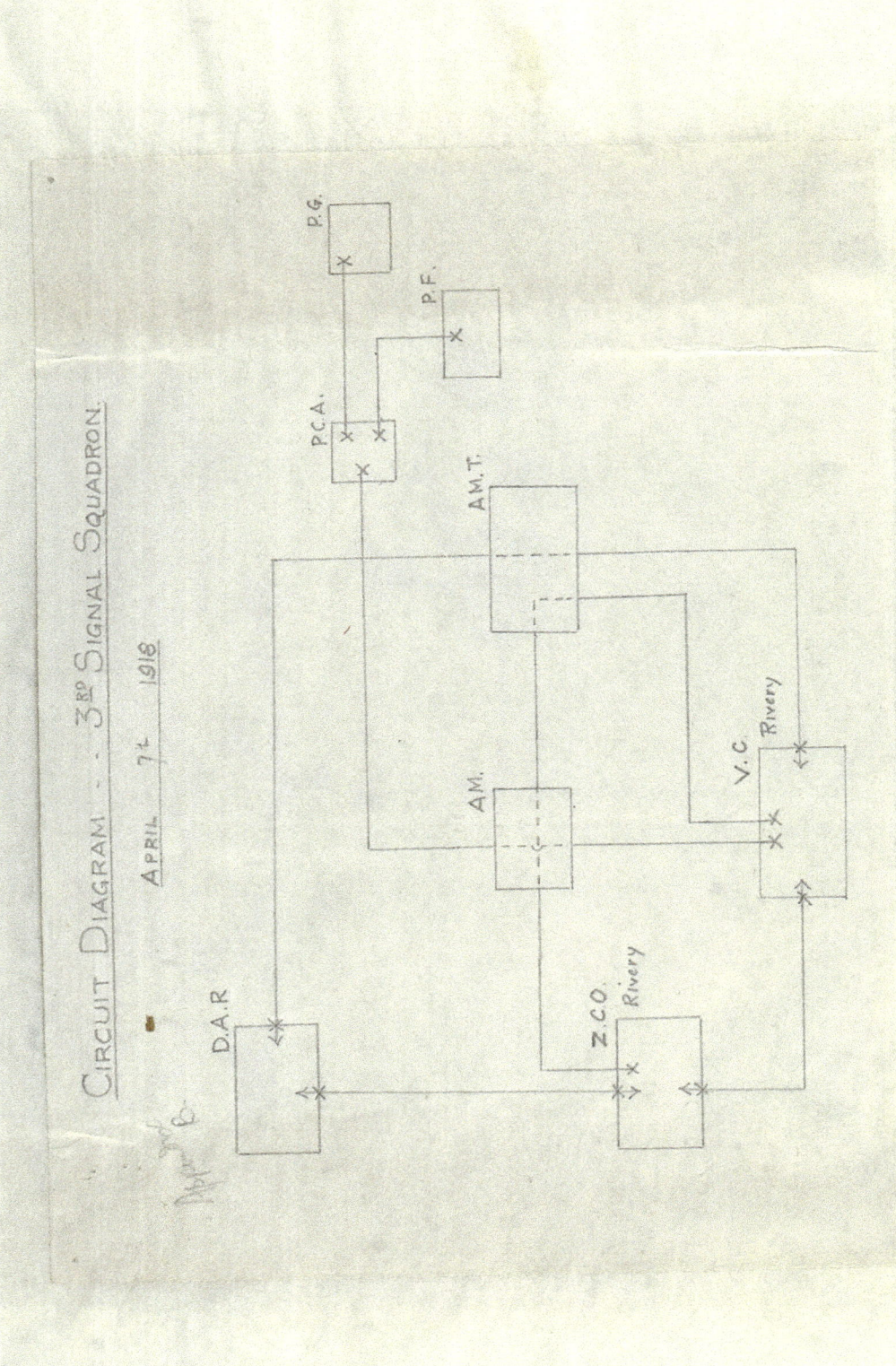

CIRCUIT DIAGRAM OF COMMUNICATIONS

V.C - - - - - APRIL 8TH 1918.

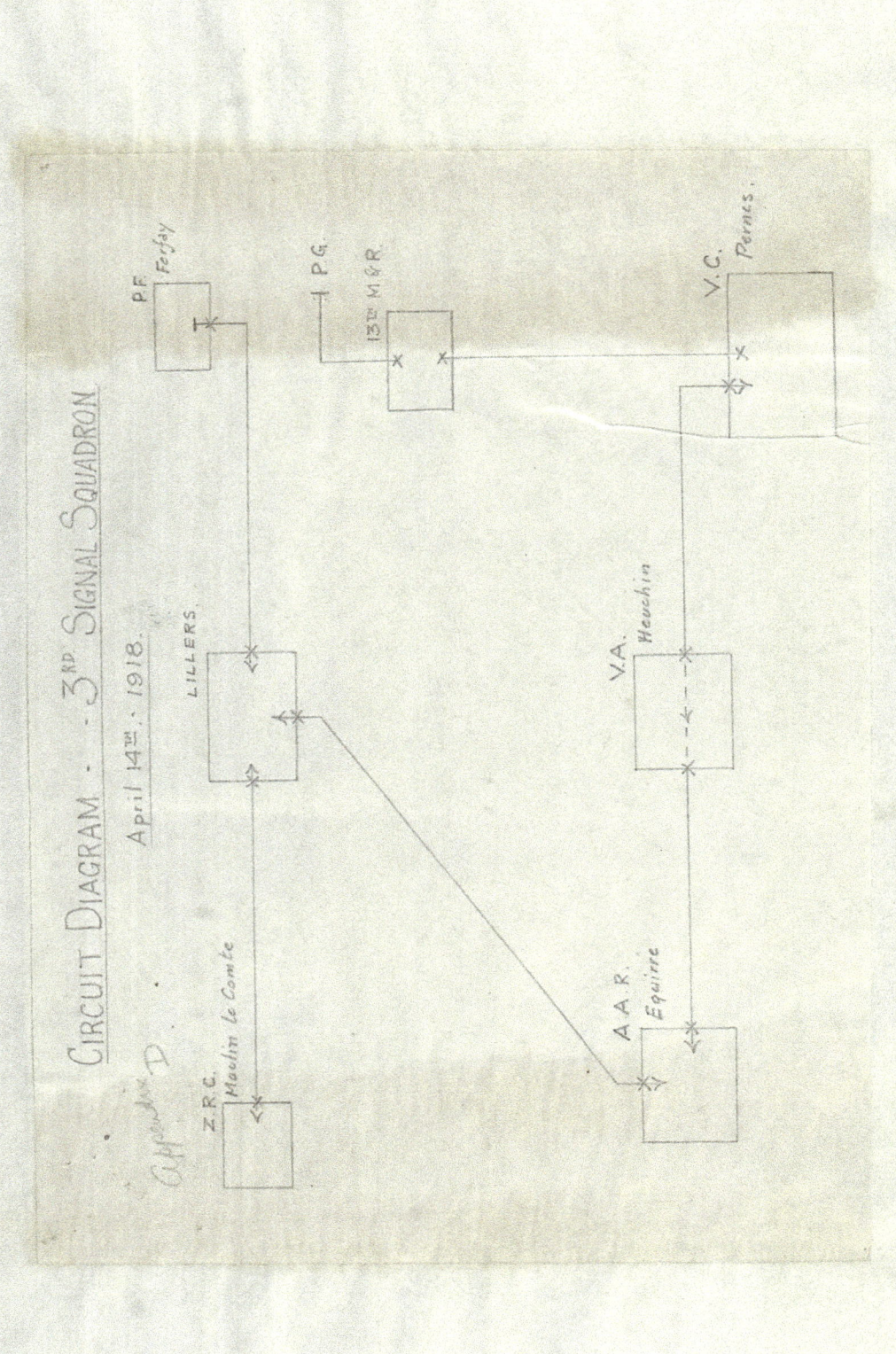

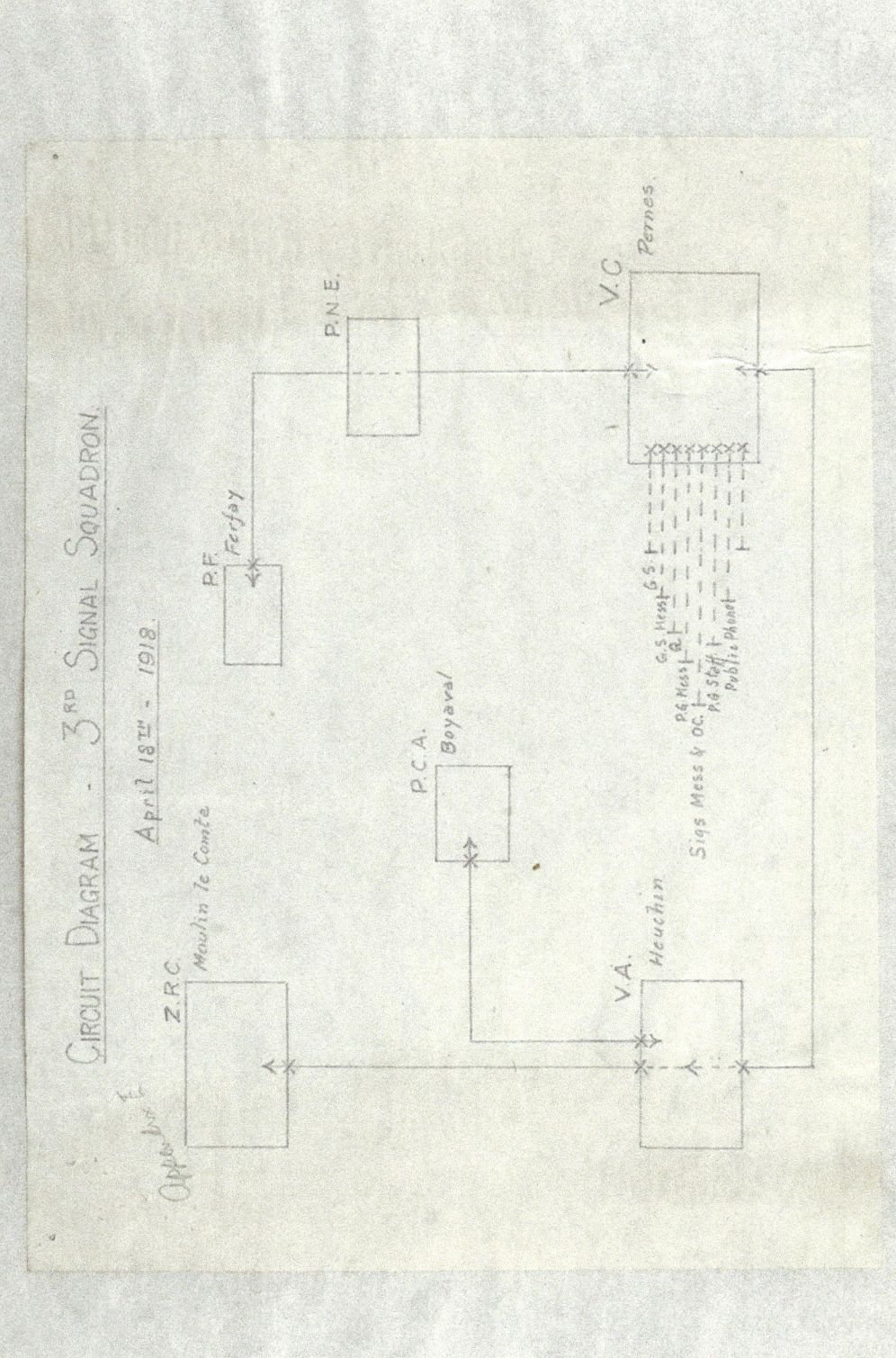

WAR DIARY or INTELLIGENCE SUMMARY

Army Form C. 2118.

MAY 1918

3rd Signal Sqdn RE

Vol 4

Place	Date	Hour	Summary of Events and Information	Remarks and references to Appendices
PERNES	1st / 2nd		Squadron continued training. Schemes with No 6 Squadron and Flight R.A.F. and Rodeo with Popham Panel and Lucas lamp.	Appendix 1.
	3rd		CAPT. C.H. HENRY assumed command 7th Signal Troop vice Lt D.A. GEARD & Rgt Sgt.	
WAIL	4th	12.30 am	order received to march to WAIL. Close down PERNES 1.50 pm. Reopen WAIL 12 noon.	
			Morse and telephone to CAR.	
YVRENCH	5th	1.50 pm	Close down WAIL. 12 noon. Reopen YVRENCH. Morse and telephone to 2CO.	
CONTAY	6th	4.25 pm	Close down YVRENCH.	
		2.15 pm	1 OR from 38 DIV. CONTAY.	
		3.35 pm	Thro' to CCO on phone.	
		5.45 pm	Thro' to 2.CO Supplepost.	
		1.40 pm	7th Cav Reg on phone	
	7th	3.15 pm	Lt Cav Reg " " CONTAY	Appendix 2.
		3.50 pm	with RAF.	
	8th		Intercept Officer Green on VC exchange. ADMS. 18th Div (BAVELINCOURT) NORTHUMBERLAND H&RS (CONTAY) 38 DIV (TOUTENCOURT) 47th DIV (BEAUCOURT). 3 Coy 9 Bn TANK CORPS. 3 Coy 3 Bn TANK CORPS. 3rd Bn (BEHENCOURT)	
	9th	6.15 pm	Cav. Cav. Reg on Morse.	
		8.5 pm	3. Field Sqdn on Phone.	
	10/14		No change.	
	15th		2nd Brig to C.C.O.	
	16th		47th DIV informed telephone over. All wires over to chancel over.	Appendix 3.
	17th	10 am	Close down CONTAY. Reopen YZEUX. Cav Reds renewed at BEHENCOURT.	
		9.30 am	BAR Superimposed	
		9.45 am	PF. Superimposed (BILLOT)	
		9.57 pm	PG. " (ST OUEN) BAR into medals	
	18/23		No change. Squadron Training.	
	24th		PEA to STOUEN, PG to BEHENCOURT	
	25/30		No change.	
	31		PF to BEHENCOURT, PGA to BELLOY	

Alex Duff Capt RE

3rd Signal Sqdn R.E.

31/6/18

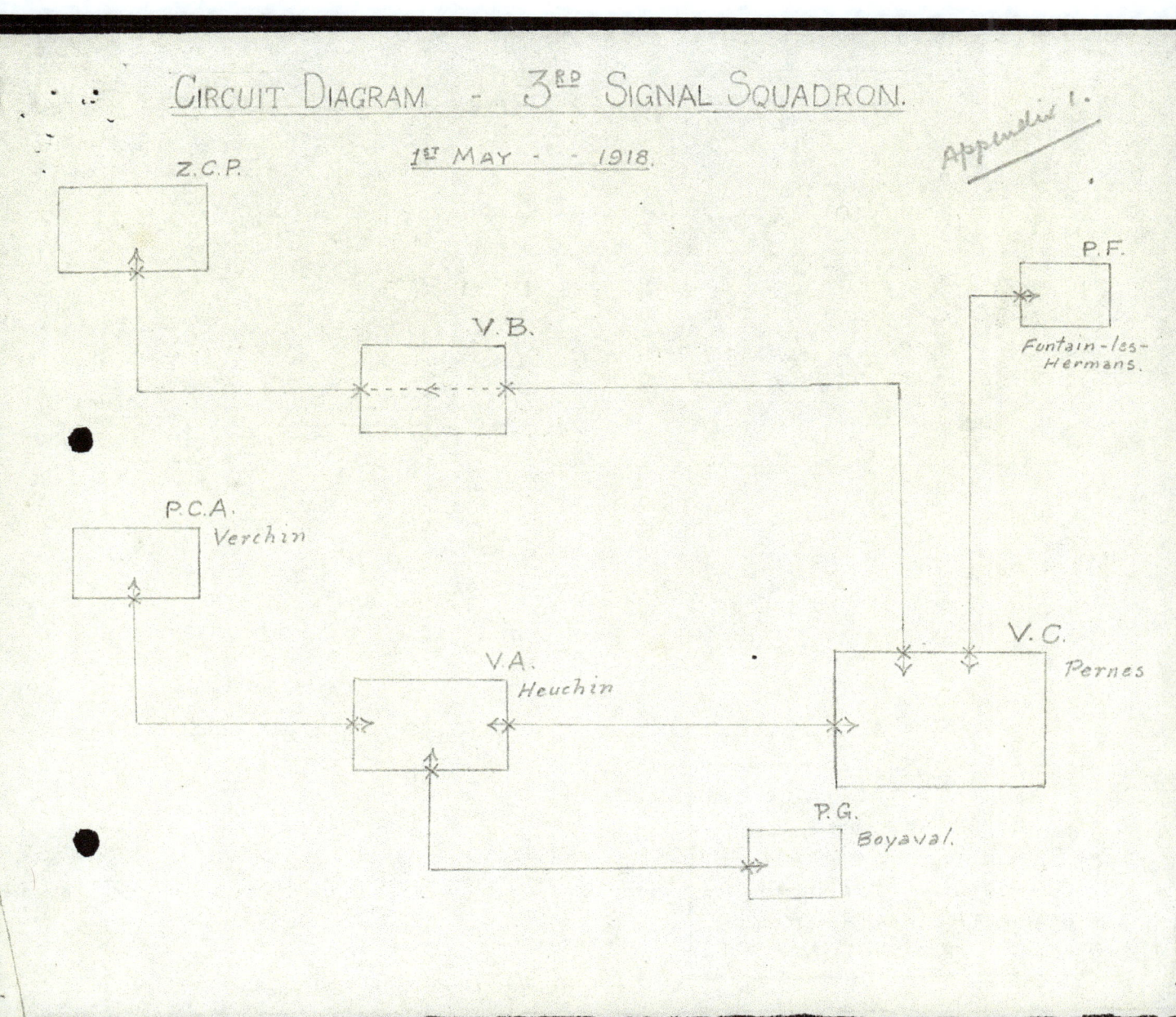

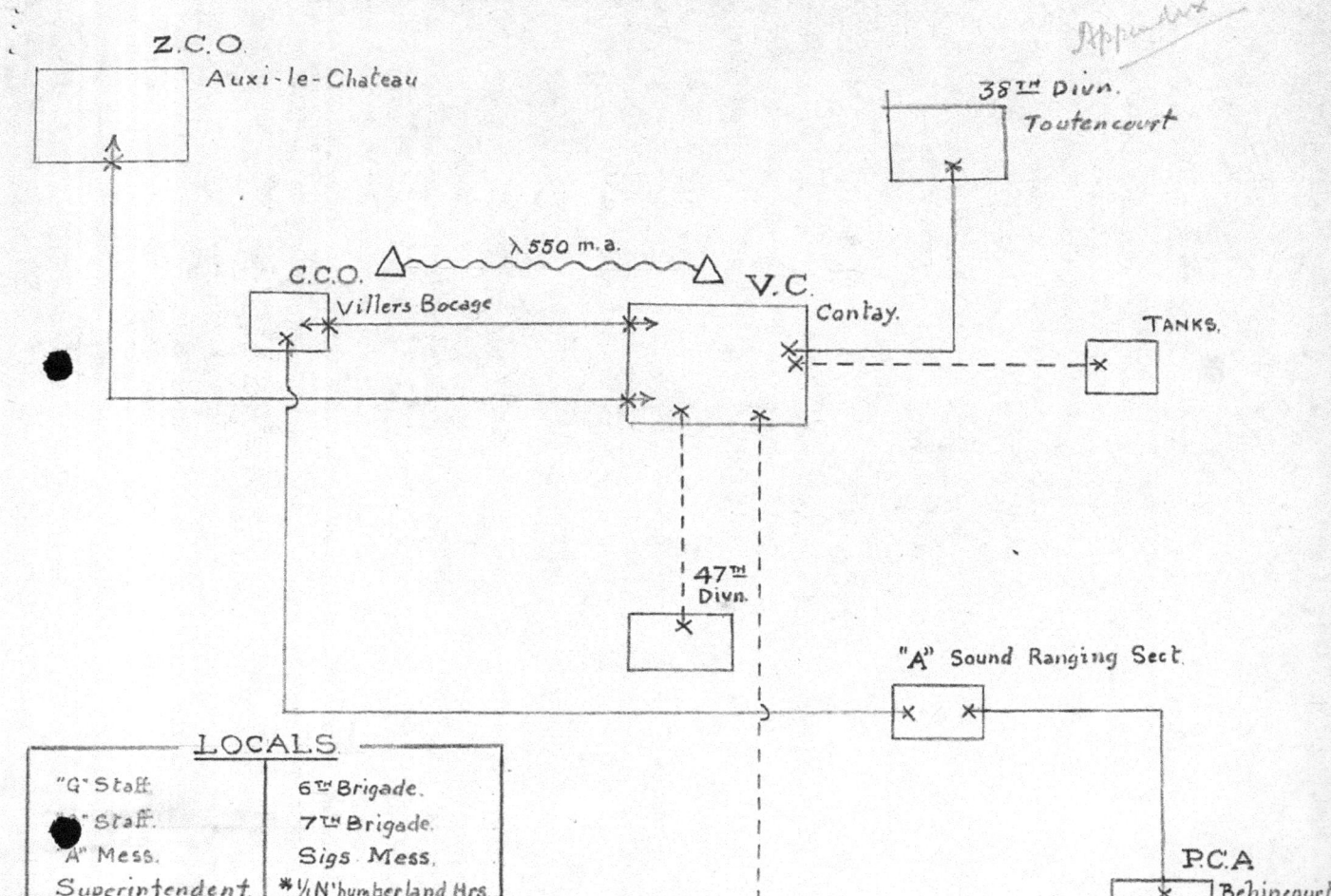

Circuit Diagram of Communications.
3rd Cavalry Division ~ May. 10th, 1918.

Appendix 3

Z.C.O. — Auxli-le-Chateau.

38th Divn. — Toutencourt.

3rd Batn. Tanks.

1/ N'humberland Hrs. — Vadencourt.

"C" Coy, 3rd Btn. — Tanks — "C" Coy. 9th Btn. — Warley.

K.X.D. — 1/ London Regt.

18th Divn. — Bavelincourt.

P.C.A — 3rd Fd.Sqdn. — Behencourt.

V.C. — Contay.

47th Divn. — Beaucourt.

C.C.O — Villers Bocage. — λ 550 m.a.

LOCALS
- "G" Staff.
- "Q" Staff.
- "A" Mess
- Sigs Mess.
- 4th Brigade R.H.A. Office and Mess.
- 6th Brigade.
- 7th Brigade.
- A.D.M.S
- Superintendent

All Circuits truly Metallic.

R.J. Brancliff, Capt.
Comdg. 3rd Signal Squadron, R.E

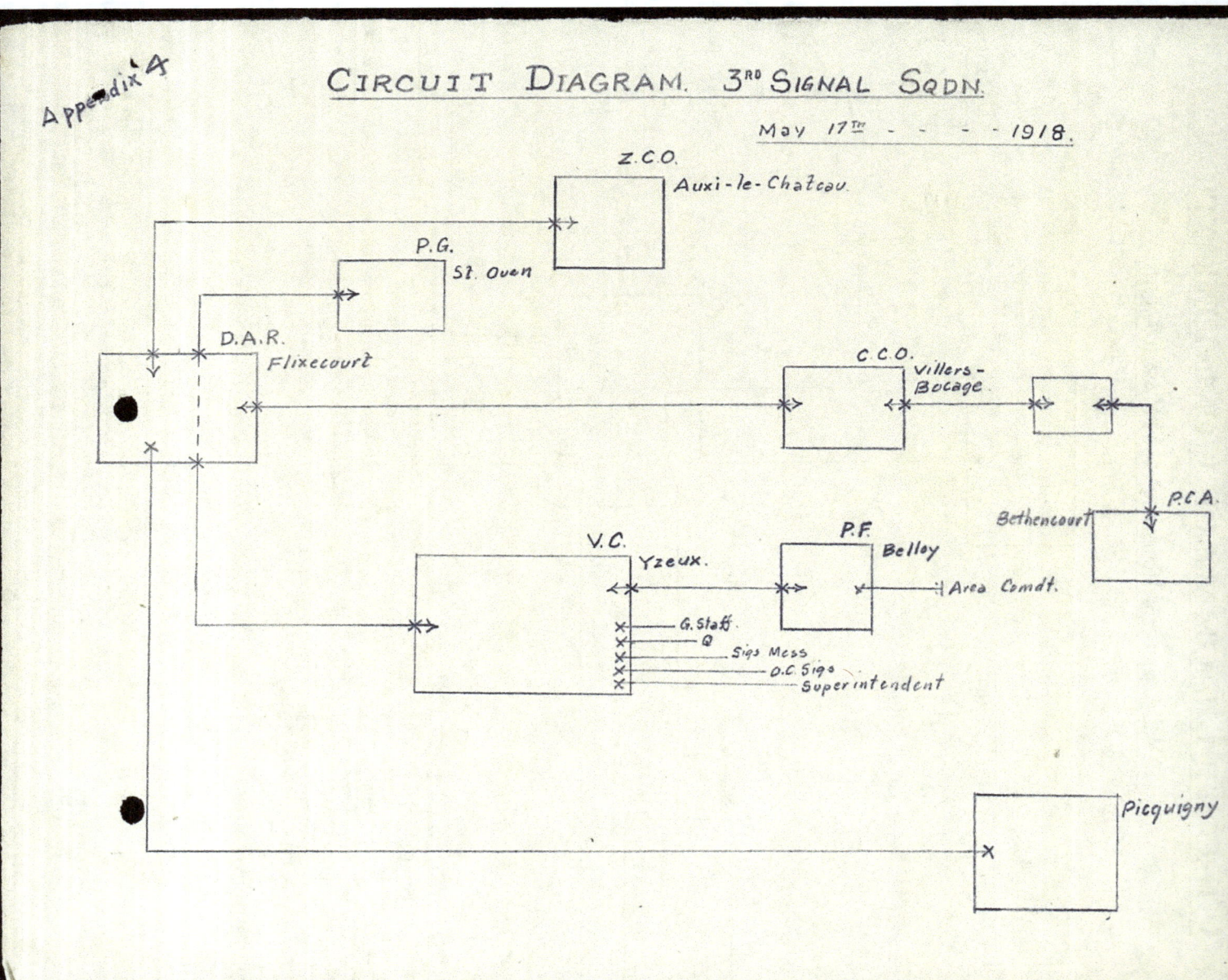

WAR DIARY or INTELLIGENCE SUMMARY

Army Form C. 2118.

3rd Signal Squadron R.E.

JUNE 1918

Place	Date	Hour	Summary of Events and Information	Remarks and references to Appendices
YZEUX	1/31		Routine duties and parades as usual. Visits in Esston continued.	
	2nd			
	3rd-9th		Trumpeters to 6th Cav. Bde. Cinedrome Phoult. 58th Division.	
	10th		School spell by Regiment. aug. Brigade 7 Division training Personnel, and those returned to 6th Cav. Bde. for duties on to 3rd Corps 7 Exchange.	
	11th-13th		Squadron parades and trained as before. Lecture by Medical officer on 1st Aid.	
	14th		7th Cav. Bde. closed down BELLOY 7:45am, Reopen Bulscourt 12:5pm. 6th Cav. Bde. open BELLOY 9:50am.	
	15/16th		Asstonals attended Brigade scheme with Canadian Bde. Squadron paraded for inspection at 9am in full marching order.	
	17th		Usual Parades and duties. Brigade scheme, with aeroplane and W/T (lent by Cav. Corps) included, carried out by Squadron and 1st and 7th Cav. Regts. W/T worked excessively well, messages being sent through to Peter in Cipher.	Appendix I.
	18th/19th		7th Cav. Bde. Classification of Signalmen as are expected Squadron transport 9:30am. 10.K.	
	20/21		No change.	
	22.		Cav. Corps. Bde. Closed down St. OUEN 7am. Reopen Bulscourt 11:45-2 Am. 7th Cav. Bde. open St OUEN 11:5am.	
	23, 24		No change.	
	25. 26.	10.30 am	6th Cav. Bde. Closed down BELLOY 10 am, to LE MESGE. BELLOY exch worked by Division. Telephone to 6th Cav. Bde. through 4th Army.	
	27, 28		No change.	
	29.	9.15pm	4th ABde RHA Closed down BELLOY. Proposed later at POULAINVILLE.	Appendix II.
	30.		4th Bde RHA to 4th Australian Division.	

Alban Croft Capt.
3rd Signal Squadron R.E.

Circuit Diagram 3rd Signal Squadron R.E. 22-6-18.

Appendix. I.

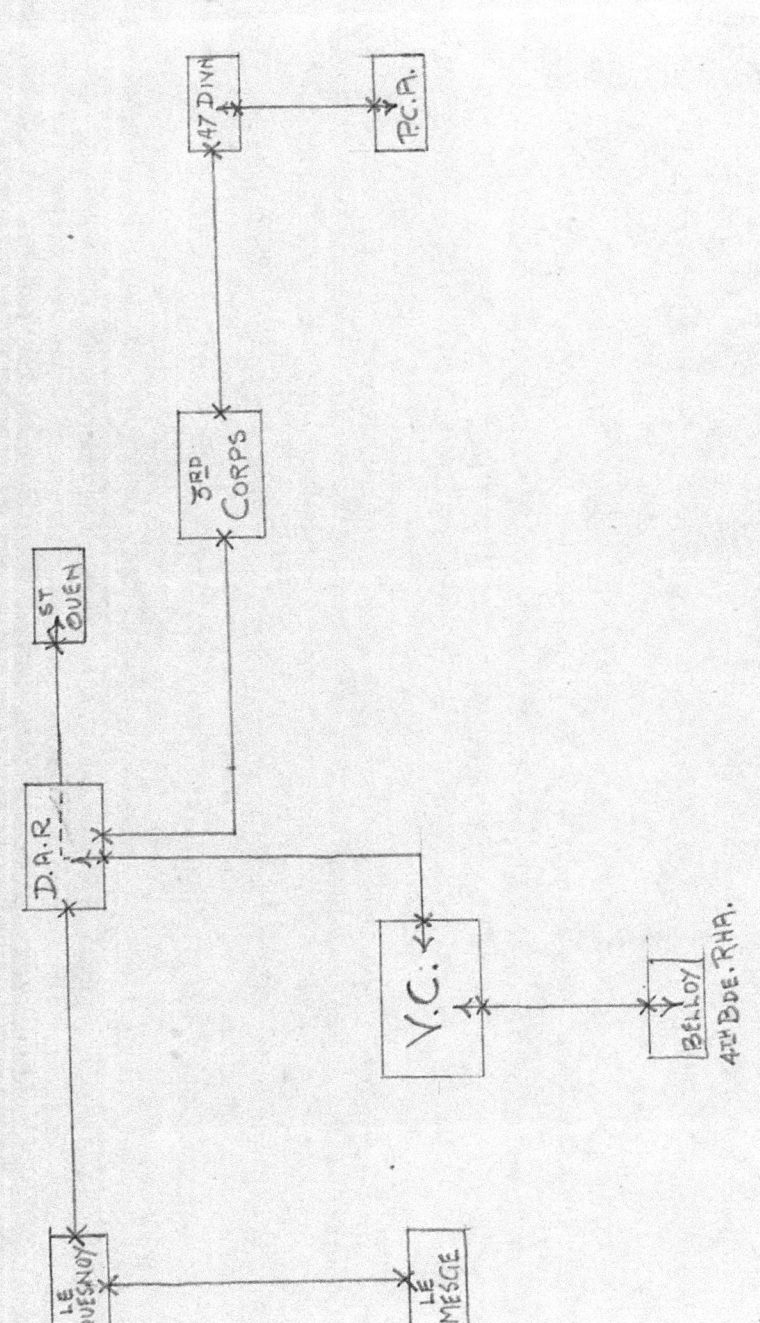

2. 29.6.18

CIRCUIT DIAGRAM 3RD SIGNAL SQUADRON, R.E.

APPENDIX II

29.6.18.

- ST OUEN
- 4TH AUS. DIVN.
- 4TH BDE. R.H.A.
- AUST. CORPS
- D.A.R.
- R.T.C.G. EX.
- P.C.A.
- V.C.
- BELLOY
- LE QUESNOY
- LE MESGE

WAR DIARY
or
INTELLIGENCE SUMMARY.

(Erase heading not required.)

3rd Signal Sqdn. R.E.

July 15.8.

Place	Date	Hour	Summary of Events and Information	Remarks and references to Appendices
YZEUX	1st/2nd		No change.	
	4th		5th Army Aux Horse Transpt put on the telephone.	
	5th	11.30am	Cav. Cav. Bde opened at HANGEST-SUR-SOMME. Telephone only via 4th Army.	
	6th/15th		No change.	
			Training. No very much interfered with owing to an outbreak of P.U.O in the Division. No unit has fully furnished an Fxc. Cable occurred.	
	16th	10.53 am	Mrs Pair Munts to D.A.R.	
	17th	11.10am	Thro' circuit to PCA on 'phone	
		11.23 am	Thro' circuit to PCA Superimposed.	
	18th		No change	
	19th	11.45am	BELLOY Exch Cut out: Thro' circuit to Area Council BELLOY (2 wires)	
		12.15pm	Div.l Hospital Cut out: Thro' circuit to 6th C.F.A. (3 wires)	
	20th		No change	
	21st		6th CSA closed down BELLOY. Circulation now via 6th Cav Rec.	
	22nd/25		No change. Classification of telephones Given out.	
	26th		No change.	
	27th	11.20 a	Direct to 7th Cav Bde via ACQUIGNY.	
	28th/29		No change.	
	30th		3rd Field Sqn to BETHENCOURT ST-OUEN.	
	31st		No change.	

J Watson Capt.
Capt.

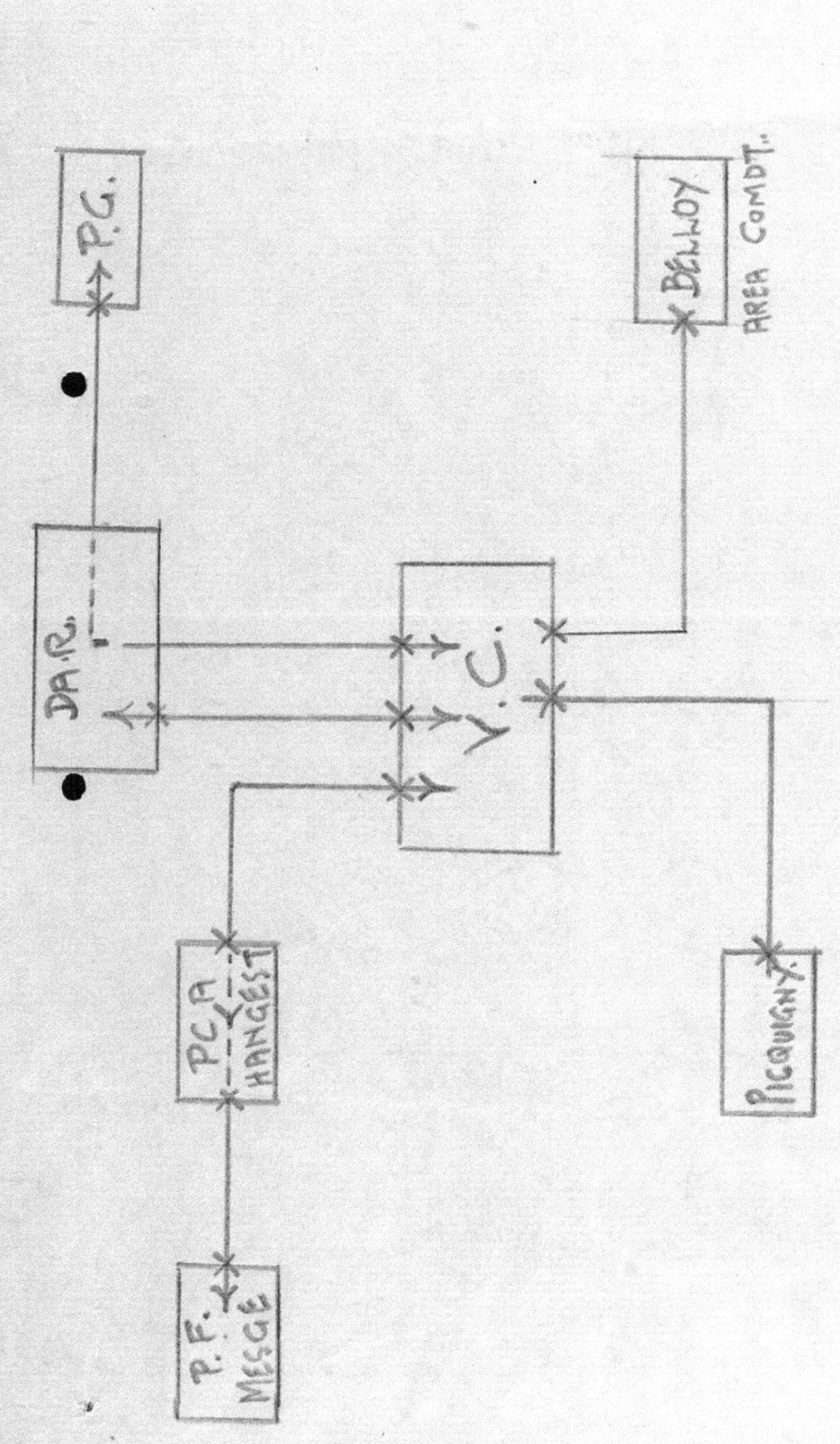

Communication 3rd Cavalry Division.
July 31st 1918.

WAR DIARY or **INTELLIGENCE SUMMARY**
Army Form C. 2118.

3RD SIGNAL SQUADRON R.E.
No. ....
Date ...12.9.18

3rd Signal Sqdn. ...... August 1918

Place	Date	Hour	Summary of Events and Information	Remarks and references to Appendices
YZEUX	1st		Lt. R.B. ROOVERMAN North Somerset Yeo joined for his Section	
	2nd/4th		Change to Indoor Branching - Electricity and Magnetism carried out.	
	5th	7.30pm	B.T. Cable Section joined from 9th Corps.	
	6th	4 AM	H/T Section (Sgt Ruislep) reported for duty from 6th Corps.	
			B.T. Cable Section moved to LONGEAU to build from LONGEAU Gate to CACHY.	
		8pm	ZCP (CAV CORPS ADV) opened YZEUX.	
		9pm	VCR opened PONT DE METZ	
		10.13pm	VCR through to CAVALRY CORPS	
		10.13pm	VC Closed down YZEUX	
		10 pm	VC Closed down PONT DE METZ Reopened on BOVES. BLANGY TRONVILLE ROAD (T3 B 4.5 Sheet 62D 1/40,000)	
	7th		Communication by phone to ZCP.	
	8th	5.45am	VCR moved to CACHY plans & ZCP.	
		7.30am	Cable established moved forward to MOGREMONT WOOD	
		9.45am	VCR moved to Southern end of MOGREMONT WOOD. H/T thro' to 2CD. Cable did not arrive up. From this point B.T. Section carried on the lines:- Southern end of Small wood South of A in IGNACOURT, thro' to Spur one mile S.W. of point 88. Cable Sec succeeded in building up cable head to their point and continued thro' report centre in main N of day. BEAUCOURT - Cross Roads 2 miles NE of CAYEUX WOOD. S.67 CAYEUX WOOD. J up to this point. Commn also R.C. then moved to CAYEUX WOOD - Cross Roads on Cross Roads in by Visual.	
		8.30pm	Bivouacked for night Fort Pargny 1 mile S of H/T Cable, D.R., and on one or one cross in YEUCUT all day.	
	9th	10.45am	Sn Rpt to 2CP by means of H/T Cable, DR.	
			R.C. moved to CAYEUX WOOD on CAIX - CAYEUX Road.	
	10th	5.30am	moved to E.16 D. CAIX by phone to 2CP. } Communication & ZCP by phone and K/T Central DR. forwarded by Red DR.	
		12.30pm	" Windmill in	
		2.30pm	" E.28 A Central.	
		4.45pm	" K 11 Central.	
		8.0pm	" K 36 76 are Divisional for night	

Army Form C. 2118.

WAR DIARY
or
INTELLIGENCE SUMMARY.
(Erase heading not required.)

Instructions regarding War Diaries and Intelligence Summaries are contained in F.S. Regs., Part II and the Staff Manual respectively. Title pages will be prepared in manuscript.

Place	Date	Hour	Summary of Events and Information	Remarks and references to Appendices
BOVES	11th	6.30pm	Remained in bivouac all and cloud down 6.30pm.	
			Leopard BOVES CAVROIT 6.30pm.	
		7.30pm	" BOVES CHAU - BOIS DE BOVES.	
	12th	1pm	on phone to 2CP at ST FUSCIEN	APPENDIX I
			on phone to Canadian Cav. Bde. Le PARACLET	
SAINS EN AMIENOIS	13th	4pm	Cloud down BOVES	
		4pm	Reopened SAINS EN AMIENOIS.	
	14th		PCA and PF (Le PARACLET and St FUSCIEN on phone)	
		1pm	PG on phone SAINS EN AMIENOIS	
YZEUX	15th	7pm	Close down	APPENDIX II
		7.14pm	Reopened at DAR on move	
		8.30pm	VB on phone ST OUEN.	
	16th	12.30pm	PG on phone HANGEST	
		1.20pm	PCA " phone AIMESOF	
		4.25pm	PF " phone (BELLOY)	
		4.8pm	VB Close down (BELLOY)	III
	17th	4.45pm	C.R.H.A. Opened BELLOT	
		1.25pm	B7. Cable section & LONGLEBU under 4th Army.	
	18th		3rd Cav M.T. Coy on phone - LA FOLIE - via PG.	IV
	19/20		Received Visual Signaller and Report Centre.	
	21st	8.30pm	PCA Cloud down HANGEST	
		10pm	PF Cloud down LEMESGF	
		10.30pm	B7 Cable section rejoined.	
	22nd	12.30am	PCA on phone at DOMART EN PONTHIEU.	
		2.3(am)	PG on phone at FIEFFES.	
	23rd		No change.	
	24th			

WAR DIARY
or
INTELLIGENCE SUMMARY

Army Form C. 2118.

Place	Date	Hour	Summary of Events and Information	Remarks and references to Appendices
YZEUX	25th	8pm	PF Cloud down FIEFFES.	
		7.30pm	Pg Cloud down ST OUEN.	
			PCA Cloud down DOMART EN PONTHIEU.	
		9.30pm	VC Cloud down YZEUX.	
		9.30pm	VC Reopened FONTAINE-L'ETALON.	
			Brigade all on phone thro' Cav Corps	
			PF. GUESCHART. Pg LE BOISLE. PCA BOUFFLERS.	
	26th	4pm	PF Cloud down.	
		5pm	PCA Cloud down.	
		5pm	VC Cloud down FONTAINE L'ETALON Reopened WAIL, Aux' & HESDIN.	
		8.10pm	PF on phone at NUNCQ.	
		10pm	Pg MONCHEL thro' on phone, PCA CONCHY thro' Pg	
	27th/31st		No changes in Communications. Division Remained Stationary ready to move at short notice.	

J. Monteith Capt.
3rd Scout Squadron
31/8/18.

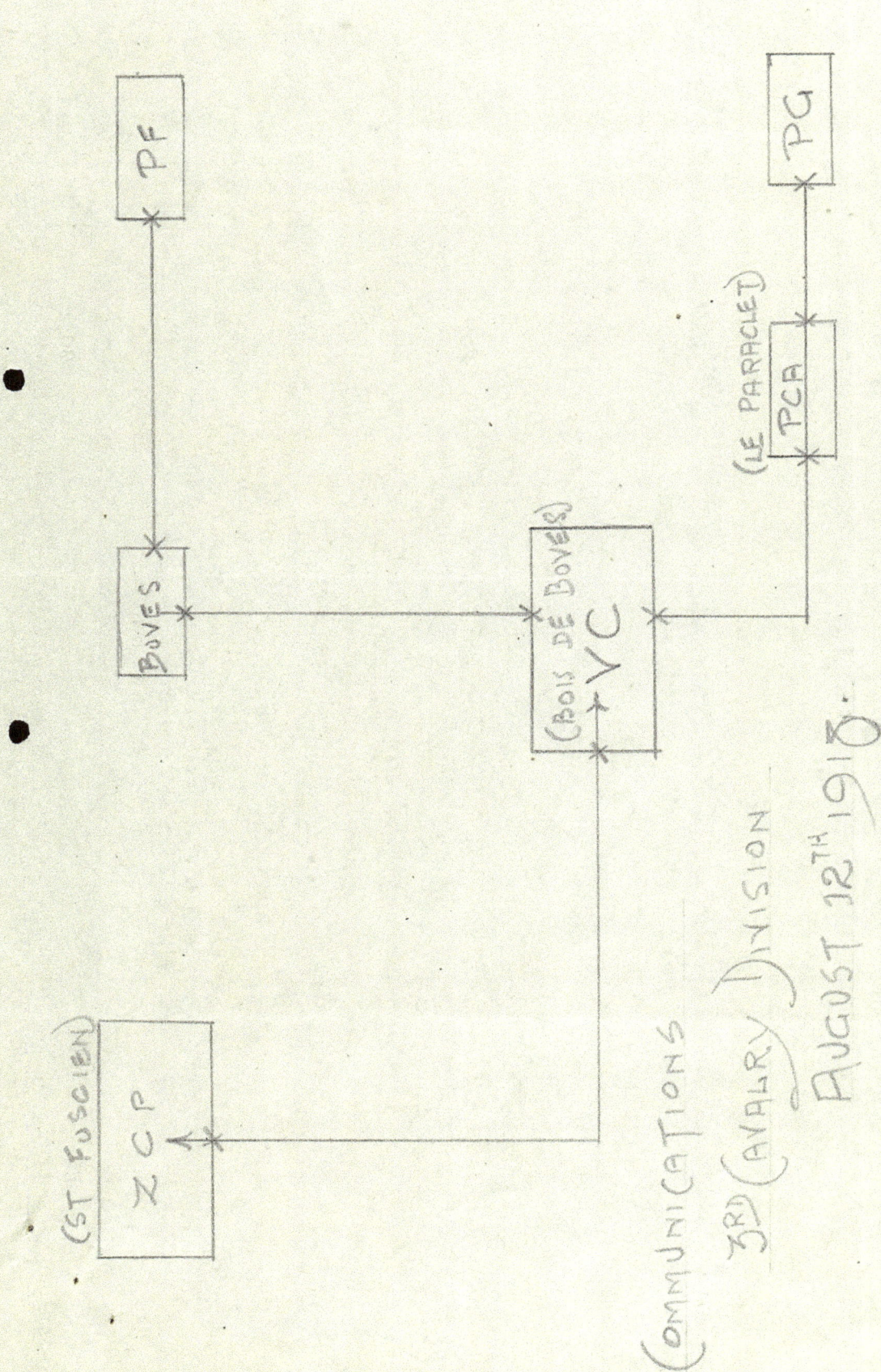

APPENDIX II

COMMUNICATIONS
3RD CAVALRY DIVISION
AUGUST 14TH 1918.

```
(ST FUSCIEN)                    (FOUENCAMPS)
 ┌─────┐                           ┌────┐
 │ ZCP │×──────→×┌────┐×──────────×│ PF │
 └─────┘         │ YC │             └────┘
                 └────┘
                 ×(SAINS EN AMIENOIS)
                  │
                  │         (GUYENCOURT)
                  │           ┌────┐
                  │         ×─│ PG │
                  │           └────┘
                  │         (LES PARACLET)
                  │           ┌─────┐
                  └─────────×─│ PCA │
                              └─────┘
```

Appendix III

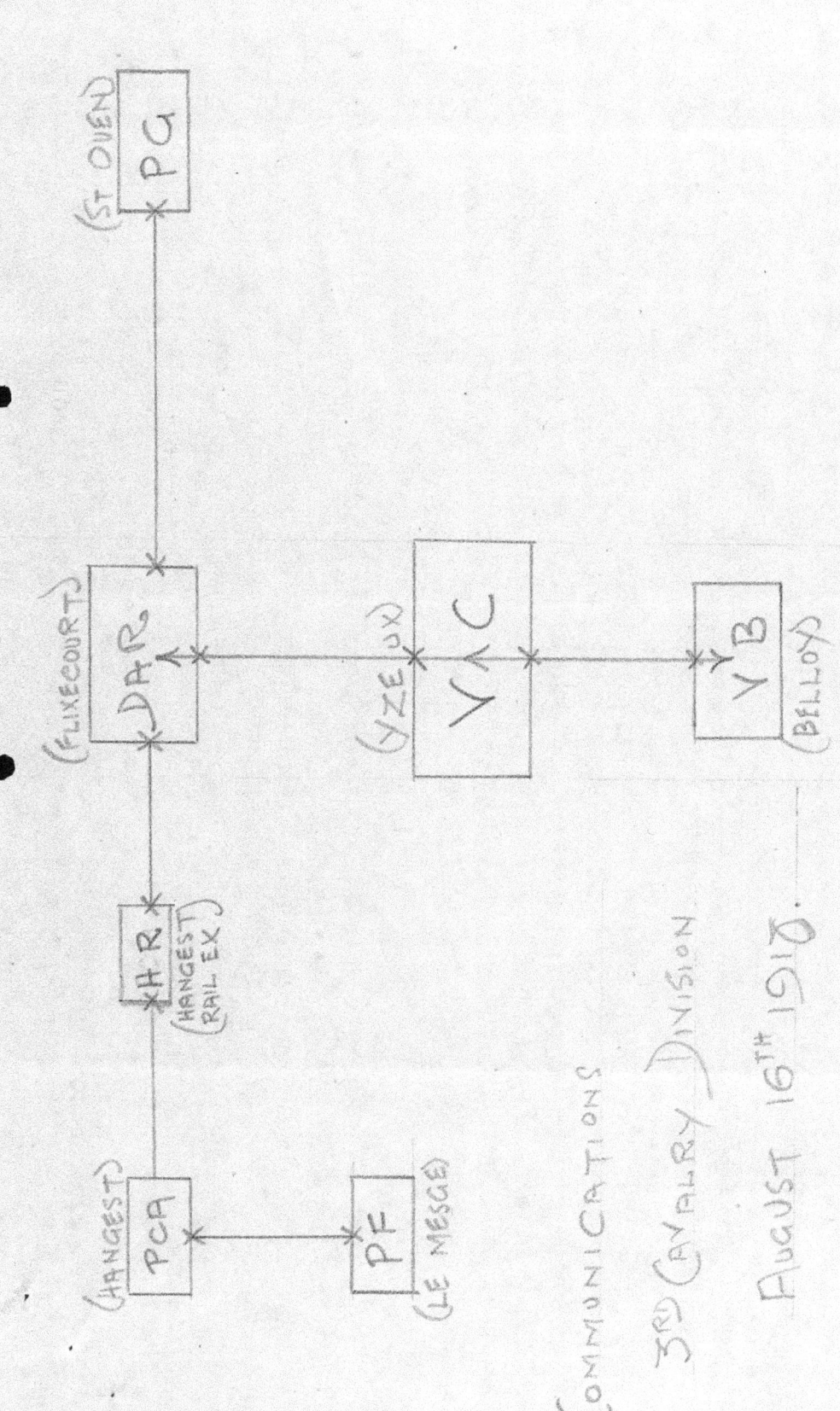

Communications
3rd (Cavalry) Division
August 16th 1917.

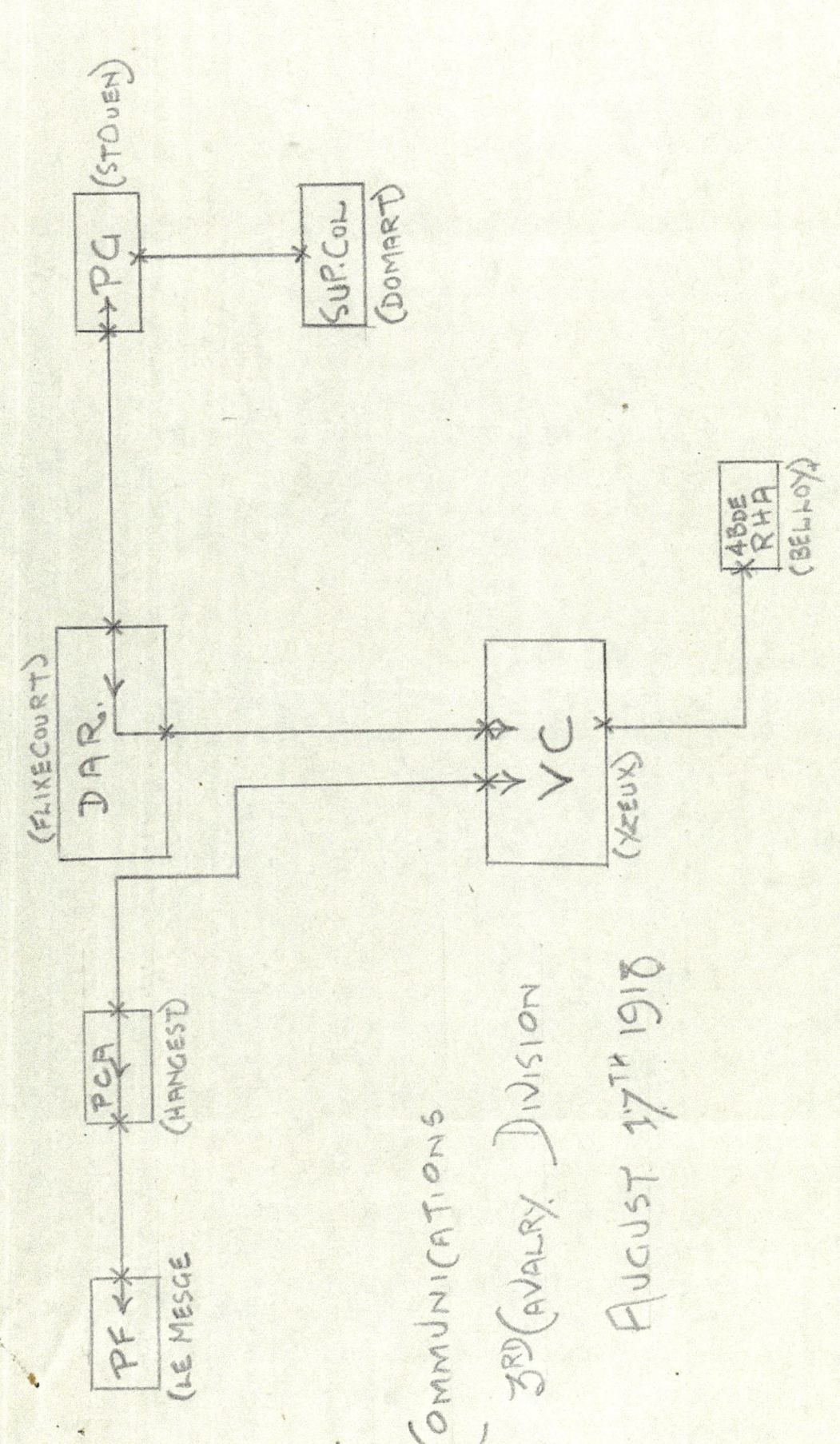

WAR DIARY or **INTELLIGENCE SUMMARY.** 3rd Siege Search Lt.

Army Form C. 2118.

Sept. 1918.

Place	Date	Hour	Summary of Events and Information	Remarks and references to Appendices
FONTAINE L'ETALON	1st/6th		No change.	
	7th	6 PM	Pg opened on 'phone at BOUBERS.	During this period the Squadron on leaving in Visual work, Mounted Dispatch riding, etc.
	8th/15		No change.	
	16th	11.3 am	Following note took place. PFR to No. 12 Rue d'arras	
		11.30 am	PgR to ROLLENCOURT.	
		11.5 am	PgR A BLINGEL	
	17th		Cavalry Corps Transport.	
	18th		Bde moved back into new DA area.	
	19th	8.25 am	Redistribution of area. Pg TyILLEMAN.	
		12.51 pm	PF DEBEAUVE phone via Divert.	
		12.5 pg	PgA BOUBERS phone via "	
	20th/24th		No change.	
	25th	7 pm	Ve moved to MARIEUX (link over from VA.)	
		8 pm	phone to PgA AUTHIE.	
	26th	12.3 am	Move to Pg ORVILLE.	
		7.45 am	" " PF BUS-LES-ARTOIS.	
	27th	7.50 A	Ve, moved ALBERT.	
		1.30 A	Ve to CLERY SUR SOMME.	
	28th		No change.	
	29th	5 pm	PEUILLY Office opened.	
	30th/31		No change.	

Albion Capt.
3rd Siege Search Lt.

3rd Signal Squadron RE

WAR DIARY
or
INTELLIGENCE SUMMARY

Month of October 1918   Army Form C. 2118.

Vol 45

Place	Date	Hour	Summary of Events and Information	Remarks and references to Appendices
Montbrehain? Poeuilly	1/10/18		No change	
	2/10/18		Division ordered to move to BELLENGLISE	
		8.30	Report Centre opened at X roads N. of P. in PONTRU	
		9.30	Report centre moved to bridge at BELLENGLISE	
		10.30	Rear report centre closed at POEUILLY and moved to BIHECOURT station	
		11.30	Rear report centre reopened at POEUILLY	
		12.05	Advanced rep. centre closed down BELLENGLISE Bridge, plans to Cavalry Corps rdv.	
	3/10/18	8.30	Division saddles up and ready to move at	
		9.15	Division ordered to move forward	
		11.30	Office opened at PONTRU (the TUMULUS)	
		13.00	Rear report centre closed at POEUILLY	
		14.00	Adv. office closed at the (TUMULUS) and moved forward to MAGNY-LA-FOSSE — PONTRUET road NE of MAGNY-LA-FOSSE	
		15.00	New office opened	
		16	G.O.C. arrived at TUMULUS.	
		19.00	The report centre moved back and reopened at POEUILLY. In telephone comn. with 4th Army and both Cavalry Corps (TUMULUS) and telegraphic comn. with 1st Corps at POEUILLY.	
		20.30	6th Car. Bde. opened on the line beyond advn. Cav. Corps. Cav. Corps closed down and advanced office at MAGNY-LA-FOSSE now forms a through circuit to 6th Car Bde.	

3RD SIGNAL SQUADRON R.E.
No. A 190/6
Date 14/11/18

3rd Signal Squadron RE   month of October 1918   Army Form C. 2118.

WAR DIARY
or
INTELLIGENCE SUMMARY.

(Erase heading not required.)

Instructions regarding War Diaries and Intelligence
Summaries are contained in F. S. Regs., Part II.
and the Staff Manual respectively. Title pages
will be prepared in manuscript.

Place	Date	Hour	Summary of Events and Information	Remarks and references to Appendices
Magny → Pozuilly	1/10/18		No change.	
	2/10/18		Division ordered to move to BELLENGLISE	
		8.30	Report Centre opened at X roads N. of P. in PONTRU.	
		9.30	Report Centre moved to bridge at BELLENGLISE	
		10.30	Rear report centre closed at POZUILLY and moved to BIHECOURT station.	
		11.30	Rear report centre reopened at POZUILLY	
		12.05	Advanced rep. centre closed down BELLENGLISE Bridge, plus 15 Cavalry Corps only.	
	3/10/18	8.30	Division saddled up and ready to move at	
		9.15	Division trained to move forward	
		11.30	Office opened at PONTRU (the TUMULUS)	
		13.00	Rear report centre closed at POZUILLY	
		14.00	Adv. office closed at the (TUMULUS) and moved forward to MAGNY-LA-FOSSE—	
			PONTRUET road NE of MAGNY-LA-FOSSE.	
		15.00	New office opened	
		16	G.O.C. remained at TUMULUS.	
		19.00	The report centre moved back and reopened at POZUILLY.	
			In telephone line with 4th Army and Cav Cavalry Corps (TUMULUS)	
			and telegraphic line with 15th Corps at POZUILLY.	
		20.30	6th Cav Bde. opened on the line beyond adv. Cav. Corps	
			Adv. Cav Corps closed station and advanced office at MAGNY-LA-FOSSE	
			was kept through direct to 6th Cav Bde.	

Army Form C. 2118.

WAR DIARY
or
INTELLIGENCE SUMMARY.
(Erase heading not required.)

Instructions regarding War Diaries and Intelligence Summaries are contained in F.S. Regs., Part II. and the Staff Manual respectively. Title pages will be prepared in manuscript.

Place	Date	Hour	Summary of Events and Information	Remarks and references to Appendices
PREUILLY	4/10/18 5/10/18 6/10/18 7/10/18	12.30	Cdn Cav Bde were in telephone wire with in rear with 24th Bde who accepted telegrams	No change
MAGNY-la-Fosse	8/10/18	06.00	Batn. Officer departed at TUMULUS and in wire with Adv. Cav. Corps by phone	
		09.30	New officer closed down. New Office opened at 4.19 central.	
ESTRÉES		10.54	Adv office moved forward opened at N.E. end of ESTRÉES.	
		10.06.	In telephone wire with Adv. Cav. Corps, also by runner & Th. 1st Cav. Divn.	
		11.04	1st Cav Div came off the line & go forward giving us direct wire with Cadre Cav. Corps.	
		11.40	2nd Cav Div came in the line again we became intermediate between these new Cavalry Corps.	
		12.14	Battalion Divnl. wire with Adv. Cav. Corps and 6th Cav Bde	
		17.35	Adv. H.Q. Cavalry Corps moved back 15 cul farm N. of MAGNY-la-Fosse.	
Ht MAGNY-la Fosse		20.50	Line in at Est. Estress to TUMULUS (Cav Corps Adv) with 4th Guards Bde intermediate working merrily	(7 m beyond MT. PREUX)
	9/10/18	5.30	Adv. H.Q. Cav. arrived at Farm at C7.A	
		7.00	Line to Adv. Cav. Corps by phone & wire.	
		9.40.	Adv party arrived at U26.B.5.0. In telephone wire with Adv Cav Corps, also Cav Bde, by horse	
		10.48	closed down new offices opened at 11 am at C.7.A.	
		10.45	Closed down at U.26.B.8.0.	
		11.19.	Bde party opens up at 11.15 9.9	
		13.23.	In line with Adv Cav Corps by horse & phone	
		14.3	Moving wire to Adv. Cav. Corps & 6th Cav. Bde (Valley S. of MARETZ)	
		15.50	Office closed down	
	10/10/18	6.00	Report cavalry at P4.B.5.0 near MT PREUX	
			In wire with adv Cavalry Corps at MARETZ by phone & horse.	
		19.30	Cav Corps both with our office	

A.7.09T. W.W.1285.g/M12593. 750,000. 1/17. D.D & L. Ltd. Forms/C2118/14

WAR DIARY or INTELLIGENCE SUMMARY

Army Form C. 2118.

Place	Date	Hour	Summary of Events and Information	Remarks and references to Appendices
BEUVRY	4/10/18	12.30	Can. Cav. Bde. were in telephone wire with in the 24th Bde. who accepted telegrams	
	5/10/18		No change	
	6/10/18		"	
	7/10/18		"	
MARRY-la-FOSSE ESTRÉES	8/10/18	06.00	Bde. Office opened at TUMULUS and in wire with adv. Cav. Corps. by phone	
		09.30	New office opened at H.19 central	
		10.54	Bde. Office moved forward and opened at N.E. sur of ESTRÉES.	
		10.66	In telephone wire with adv. Cav. Corps., also by motor & The 1st Cav Divn. comn in wire with	
		11.04	1st Cav Divn. comn. off to line rg0 forward giving no clearer wire with adv. Cav. Corps.	
		11.40	3rd Cav Divn. came on the line again more to gain information	
		12.14	Established wired wire with adv. Cav. Corps and 6th Cav Bde	
		17.35	Adv. Sup. Cmdt moved back 15 old position N. of MARNY-LA-FOSSE.	
		20.50	Line on old tothers to TUMULUS (Cav Corps adv) with 4th Grenade Bde intermediate working heavy phone	
MARNY-la-FOSSE	9/10/18	5.30	Adv. H.q. unit arrived at farm at C7A	
		7.00	Wire to adv. Cav Corps by phone motor	
		9.40	Adv. party arrived at U26 R 8.0. in telephone wire with adv. Cav. Corps., also Cav Corps Rely by motor	
		10.08	Clear of drawn vian mp. south at Fm at C7A. (7m beyond MT. PREUX)	
		10.46	Clear of drawn at U26 R 8.0.	
		11.19	Adv. party forms up at H.D.9.9	
		12.23	In wire with Adv. Cav Corps by motor phone	
		11.43	Wired wire to adv. Cav Corps. 6th Cav Bde (Valley S. of MARETZ)	
		15.50	Office closed down	
	10/10/18	6.00	Advance parties at P.4 B.6.0 near MT. PREUX	
			In wire with Adv. Cavalry Corps. at MARETZ by phone motor.	
		9.30	Cav Corps. leather line own office.	

WAR DIARY
or
INTELLIGENCE SUMMARY
(Erase heading not required.)

Army Form C. 2118.

Place	Date	Hour	Summary of Events and Information	Remarks and references to Appendices
TROISVILLES	10/10/18	15.15	Report event closed down & moved to O.11.D.5.8 in CLARY-CAUDRY road	
		18.40	In cue with adv Cav Corps by means phone, through 4th Guards Rob Office	
		20.00	In cue with Cav Cav Rob by means of phone.	
	11/10/18		No change	
	12/10/18		Again no change	
	13/10/18	14.30	Rep. event opened at ELINCOURT.	
ELINCOURT		19.30	In telephone comm. cue with adv Cav Corps.	
		20.18	In cue with Cav Cav Rob with bworas & phone.	
	14/10/18		Report cable moved to HENNOIS Wood	
HENNOIS Wood.		11.10	In cue with 1st 13th Corps by phone. This is when Cav Corps went to.	
		12.30	Working direct to Cav Corps by phone.	
		13.56	In cue with Cav Corps	
		20.00	Working telephone thence to direct 16 Third Army.	
	15/10/18	19.26	In cue with Cav Cav Bob by telephone	
		19.58	In telephonic cue with 7th Cav Rob also 6th Cav Rob	
			We had moves cue together ooth afternoon & Cav Cav Rob (YPRES), 7th Cav Rob. (BERTINCOURT) 6th Cav Rob (HENNOIS Wood)	
			No change for the rest of the month.	

A.B. Young
Capt.
Cmd. 3rd SIGNAL SQUADRON, R.E.

WAR DIARY
or
INTELLIGENCE SUMMARY.

Army Form C. 2118.

Place	Date	Hour	Summary of Events and Information	Remarks and references to Appendices
TROISVILLES	10/10/18	15.15	Report centre closed down & moved to O.11.D.5.8. nr CLARY - CAUDRY road	
		18.40	In line with auto Cav Corps by lines 4phone, through 4th Cav Bde Office	
		20.00	In line with Cav Cav Bde by lines & phone	
	11/10/18		no change	
	12/10/18		Again no change	
ELINCOURT	13/10/18	14.30	Rep. centre opened nr ELINCOURT.	
		19.20	Day telephone line with Cav Cav Bde with across Cav Corps.	
		20.18	In line with Cav Bde with across Cav Corps phone.	
HENNOIS WOOD	14/10/18		Report centre moved to HENNOIS Wood	
		11.10	In line with 1st 13th Corps by phone, this is astern Cav Corps went to.	
		12.30	Working direct to Cav Corps by phon.	
		13.56	In line with Cav Corps.	
		20.00	Working telephone wires to divisions 16 Third Army.	
	15/10/16	19.26	In line with Cav Cav Bde by telephone	
		19.58	In telephonic line with 7th Cav Bde also (5th Cav Bde had dinner line both soon afterwards. Cav Cav Bde (YTRES), 7th Cav Bde (BERTINCOURT) 6th Cav Bde (HENNOIS Wood).	
			No change for the rest of the month.	

A. B. Johns Lieut
for.

Army Form C. 2118.

3rd Signal Sqn "R.E."

WAR DIARY
or
INTELLIGENCE SUMMARY.
(Erase heading not required.)

November 1918.

Place	Date	Hour	Summary of Events and Information	Remarks and references to Appendices
HENNOIS WOOD	1/11/18		Communications the same as at the end of October.	
	2/11/18		No change.	
	3/11/18		No change.	
	4/11/18		No change.	
	5/11/18		No change.	
	6/11/18		Division ordered to move in a N.E. direction.	
		08.00	6th Cav Bde closed down communications. Moved to MARQUION	
		09.00	6th Cav Bde reopened at Marquion	
		08.00	Canadian Cavalry Brigade closed down & moved to BUISSY	
		9.00	Can. Cav. Bde reopened at Buissy	
		08.30	7th Cav Bde moved to SAUCHY-CAUCHY reopening line on arrival	
			Line to Bde by D.R.L.S. only.	
SAINGHEIN	7/11/18	18.00	Divisional report centre opens. Line all by D.R.L.S.	
	8/11/18	14.00	In line with Third Army circuit by phone & also by means to reach Cavalry Corps. Army Third Army to intermediate station	
	9/11/18		Attached Machine Gun Bde opened up at WAHAGNIES.	
	10/11/18	12.00	Division moved to ANTOING. Having intermediate centre at RUMES	
			Line by DR only.	
		17.30	Adv. rept centre opened at ANTOING	
		18.31	Houilers line opened.	
		8.45	Office opened at VEZON.	
	11/11/18	11.45	Close down VEZON & part autos moved to TOURPES.	

(A7562) Wt. W12839/M1303 75,000. 1/17. D.D. & L. Ltd. Forms/C.2118 14.

Army Form C. 2118.

WAR DIARY
3rd Signal Squadron R.E.
or
INTELLIGENCE SUMMARY.

November 1918

Instructions regarding War Diaries and Intelligence Summaries are contained in F.S. Regs., Part II. and the Staff Manual respectively. Title pages will be prepared in manuscript.

(Erase heading not required.)

Place	Date	Hour	Summary of Events and Information	Remarks and references to Appendices
TOURPES ANTOING	11/11/18	18.00	Report cable closed down, attached to ANTOING	
		19.00	Opened up again at ANTOING. one by wireless.	
	12/11/18		No change.	

3rd Signal Squadron R.E. WAR DIARY

INTELLIGENCE SUMMARY

November 1918

Army Form C. 2118.

Place	Date	Hour	Summary of Events and Information	Remarks and references to Appendices
ANTOING	13/11/18	08:00	Cavalry Corps leave SEELIN & go to Tour. War opening this same hour.	
		22:10	In wire with Cavalry Corps by buzz phone also division.	
	14/11/18	—	Have great trouble with lines to Cav. Corps all day.	
		24.15	In direct wire with 1st Corps.	
	15/11/18	11:25	Cavalry Rct move to another army D.R.L.S. through 15th Corps. Lines can be used in clear except by addresses.	
	16/11/18	09:25	4th Cavalry Rct shut down at TOURCOING. Lines to FRESNE.	
			Wire into 7th Cavalry Rct. at transferred from Cav Rct to 74th Divn.	
		20:04	Telegram to 7th Cav Rct circulated through 74th Division.	
BASSILLY	17/11/18		Division moved to BASSILLY. Wire to Corps + Rct. by Wireless & DRLS. Cav. Corps at SILLY	
		14:00	Divisional adv. party opened at Bassilly	
ENGHIEN	18/11/18	11:00	Divisional Report Centre moved to ENGHIEN & opened King's own wire by D.R.L. & Wireless	
EMAHIEN WATERLOO	19/11/18		Cav. Corps moved to BRAINE-le-COMPTE.	
	20/11/18		Now 2nd Army late are our office. no change	
WATERLOO	21/11/18	08:30	Divisional Report Centre moves to WATERLOO	
		11:00	Division opened centre opened at Waterloo.	
PERWEZ	22/11/18		Division moved to PERWEZ	

A.B. Johns Capt.
for O.C. 3rd Sig. Sqdn. R.E.
Cmdg.

3rd SIGNAL SQUADRON RE. WAR DIARY
INTELLIGENCE SUMMARY
DECEMBER 1918

Army Form C. 2118.

Place	Date	Hour	Summary of Events and Information	Remarks and references to Appendices
MALEVE	1/12/18	—	Communications the same as in NOVEMBER 1918.	Brussels 100 ovr
	8/12/18	—	Lt TAYLOR joined from Cav Corps Sqn. Lt DENNIS rejoined RR Cable Sec. Cme by DR'L S.	
	9/12/18	—	6th Cav Bde move to winter area.	
	12/12/18	—	Division moved to move to an area SE of HUY. Cav Corps at SPA	LIEGE 100 ovr
WARET-L'EVEQUE	15/12/18	—	"RR" Cable section proceeded to TINLOT staying at WARET-L'EVEQUE. Cmc DR'L S only except MT Parts proceeded to WARET-L'EVEQUE. W/T to Cav Corps.	
TINLOT	16/12/18	—	MT parts to TINLOT. Office opened 1200. DR'L S only except W/T to Corps. Rear office closed at MALEVE 1200.	
	17/12/18	—	Line to Corps completed (Phone + Morse). Line to Can Cav Bde at MELVILLE.	
	17/12/18	—	Line to 7th Bde at XHOS completed. Forat lines to G.T.Q and B'Hosp	
	18/12/18	—	Line to 6th Bde at WARFUSSE CHATEAU via Can Cav Bde exchange. RNA Line	
	19/12/18	—	All local lines completed	
	31/12/18	—	No change.	

Cheshire Capt.
OC 3rd Signal Sqdn RE.

3rd Signal Sqdn RE WAR DIARY or INTELLIGENCE SUMMARY.

Army Form C. 2118.

JANUARY 1919

Place	Date	Hour	Summary of Events and Information	Remarks and references to Appendices
TINLOT	1/1/19	—	Communications as in December 1918.	LIEGE & MARCHE
	9/1/19	—	W/T Set returned to Cavalry Corps.	
	9/1/19	—	Second line to 2C.O. via SRG. (Cav Corps Concentration Camp Seraing)	
	22/1/19	—	O.C. (Capt LORD (HESHAM) left for England) Captain S A LEE (Fort Garry Horse) Commanding	
	28/1/19	—	Line to Fourth Army PL RT School RAMET via SERAING Ex (sic)	
	30/1/19	—	Line to Lord Strathcona's Horse (LSH)	

S A Lee
Captain
CMDG 3rd Signal Squadron RE.

Army Form C.2118.

3rd SIGNAL SQUADRON RE WAR DIARY or INTELLIGENCE SUMMARY

FEBRUARY 1919

Place	Date	Hour	Summary of Events and Information	Remarks and references to Appendices
TINLOT	1/2/19	—	COMMUNICATIONS AS IN JANUARY 1919.	MAPS and MARCHE 1/100,000
	10/2/19	—	D.A.D.O.S. moved to ENGHIS, line to him via M.T. Coy where 5 line exchange installed.	
	10/2/19	—	CAPT STANCLIFFE commanding, having returned from ENGLAND. CAPT LEE returned to Canadian Cavalry Bde. Signal Troop.	
	11/2/19	—	Procedure Course started.	
	15/2/19	—	Line to Animal Collecting Stn (ENG1S) from PCA.	
	15/2/19	—	Procedure Course ended.	
	16/2/19 to 28/2/19		No changes in communications. Demobilisation of other ranks who could be spared continued under the orders of C.S.O.	

N Stancliffe Capt.
3rd Senior Squadron

Officer i/c
 A.Gs. Office,
 BASE.

W.D.56.

Herewith War Diary of 3rd Signal Squadron for the month of March, 1919.

Kindly acknowledge receipt.

J. H. Blackburn
                                    Captain,
                                Staff Captain,
14.4.19.   for G.O.C., 3rd Cavalry Division Cadre Brigade.

3rd Signal Squadron WAR DIARY
R.E.
or
INTELLIGENCE SUMMARY.

March 1919   Army Form C. 2118.

WD 50

Place	Date	Hour	Summary of Events and Information	Remarks and references to Appendices
TIN LOT	1/3/19		No change	
	2/3/19		Canadian Cavalry Brigade move to Canadian Corps area.	
	3/3/19		Work in lines through Villers-la-Temple – EHEIN – ENGIS, moving Wireless required by move of Canadians	
	5/3/19		No change	
	6/3/19		7th D.G's. move to 2nd Cavalry Division Area.	
	7/3/19 30/3/19		No change	
	31/3/19		3rd Signal Squadron broke up & its Cadre under Lieut A.B. Johns goes to FLEMALLE-HAUT.	

A. B. John Lieut.
O.C. 3rd Signal Squadron

www.ingramcontent.com/pod-product-compliance
Lightning Source LLC
Chambersburg PA
CBHW080850230426
43662CB00013B/2064